Important Notice

THIS BOOK IS *NOT A RETAIL PRICE LIST*

Premium prices are the average amount dealers will pay for coins (according to condition) if required for their stock.

(See page 12)

Current *retail* valuations of all U.S. coins are listed in Whitman's A GUIDE BOOK OF UNITED STATES COINS by R. S. Yeoman, Western Publishing Company, Inc., Racine, Wisconsin ($3.95).

Brief guides to grading are placed before each major coin type in this book. For those readers who desire more detailed descriptions of all coin grades, we recommend OFFICIAL A.N.A. GRADING STANDARDS FOR UNITED STATES COINS, Western Publishing Company, Inc., Racine, Wisconsin.

OFFICIAL
BLUE BOOK OF UNITED STATES COINS

1980
HANDBOOK
OF
UNITED STATES
COINS

With Premium List

By R. S. YEOMAN

THIRTY-SEVENTH EDITION

Edited by Kenneth Bressett

Containing mint records and prices paid by dealers for all U.S. coins. Information on collecting coins—how coins are produced—mints and mint marks—grading of coins—location of mint marks—preserving and cleaning coins—starting a collection—what to buy—history of mints and interesting descriptions of all U.S. copper, nickel, silver and gold coins. Fully illustrated. INDEX PAGE 128.

Whitman Coin Products

Copyright © 1979 by
WESTERN PUBLISHING COMPANY, INC.
RACINE, WISCONSIN 53404

9050-1   ISBN: 0-307-09050-7   Printed in U.S.A.

Foreword

Since 1941, annually revised editions of this Handbook have aided thousands of people who have coins to sell or are actively engaged in collecting United States coins. The popular coin folder method of collecting by date has created ever-changing premium values, based on the supply and demand of each date and mint. Through its panel of contributors the Handbook has, over the years, reported these changing values. It also serves as a source of general numismatic information to all levels of interest in the hobby.

This volume offers a helping hand to the new collector; explains what he should collect and what he should discard; tells him how to appraise and care for his coins. Explanations are fundamental, so that the reader may quickly derive the utmost in enjoyment and profit from his collection, even though it be of common coins taken from ordinary pocket change.

While the primary purpose of this volume is to smooth the path of the beginner toward numismatics, much of the information (such as mint records, premium prices, varieties, etc.) will prove invaluable to the more advanced collector.

The premium list gives representative prices paid by dealers for various United States coins. These are averages of prices assembled from many widely separated sources. On some issues slight differences in price among dealers may result from proximity to the various mints or heavily populated centers. Other factors, such as local supply and demand or dealers' stock conditions, may also tend to cause deviations from the prices listed. While many coins bring no premium when circulated, they usually bring premium prices in Uncirculated and Proof condition.

CONTRIBUTORS

Lee F. Hewitt, the former editor and publisher of the NUMISMATIC SCRAPBOOK MAGAZINE, was an early contributor, having supplied many of the historical references and explanations which appear throughout this book.

Charles E. Green gave valuable counsel when the first edition of the HANDBOOK was undertaken. He supplied most of the mint data and was a regular contributor to each revised edition until his death in 1955.

CONTRIBUTORS TO THE THIRTY-SEVENTH EDITION

Kenneth E. Bressett — *Coordinating Editor*

Kamal M. Ahwash
Michael H. Aron
Robert F. Batchelder
A. E. Bebee
Philip E. Benedetti, Sr.
George Blenker
Q. David Bowers
Philip Bressett
Hy Brown
Judy Cahn
Jerry Cohen
Ben M. Douglas
Kurt Eckstein
Chuck Furjanic
Dorothy Gershenson
Ira M. Goldberg

Lawrence S. Goldberg
Kenneth Goldman
James L. Halperin
C. Edward Hipps
Jesie Iskowitz
Curtis Iversen
Robert H. Jacobs
Floyd O. Janney
Arthur Kagin
Donald Kagin
Paul Kagin
David W. Karp
Stanley Kesselman
Mike Kliman
Abner Kreisberg
Tom McAfee

Robert T. McIntire
Fred Malone
Bill Mertes
Sylvia Novack
V. H. Oswald, Sr.
Joe Person
Joel D. Rettew
Earl C. Schill
Neil Shafer
Robert R. Shaw
Norman Schultz
Mulford B. Simons, Jr.
Maurice A. Storck, Sr.
Russel P. Vaughn
Gary L. Young

IF YOU HAVE COINS TO SELL

The publishers are not engaged in the rare coin business; however, the chances are that the dealer from whom you purchased this book is engaged in the buying and selling of rare coins—contact him first. In the event that you purchased this book from a source other than a numismatic establishment, consult your local telephone directory for the names of coin dealers (they will be found sometimes under the heading of "Stamp and Coin Dealers"). If you live in a city or town that does not have any coin dealers, it is suggested that you obtain a copy of one of the trade publications in order to obtain the names and addresses of many of the country's leading dealers.

Several popular magazines and papers are devoted to coin collecting:

COINage Magazine
16250 Ventura Boulevard
Encino, California 91316

Hobbies Magazine
1006 S. Michigan Ave.
Chicago, Ill. 60605
(Has a coin section)

Coins Magazine
Iola, Wisconsin 54945

Numismatic News Weekly
Iola, Wisconsin 54945

Coin World
P.O. Box 150
Sidney, Ohio 45365

The Numismatist
P.O. Box 2366
Colorado Springs, Colo. 80901
(Published monthly by American
Numismatic Assn.)

COLLECTING COINS

Numismatics or coin collecting is one of the world's oldest hobbies, dating back several centuries. Coin collecting in America did not develop to any extent until about 1840, as our pioneer forefathers were too busy carving a country out of wilderness to afford the luxury of a hobby. The discontinuance of the large-sized cent in 1857 caused many persons to attempt to accumulate a complete set of the pieces while they were still in circulation. One of the first groups of collectors to band together for the study of numismatics was the Numismatic and Antiquarian Society of Philadelphia, organized on January 1, 1858. Lack of an economical method to house a collection held the number of devotees of coin collecting to a few thousand until the Whitman Publishing Company and other manufacturers placed the low-priced coin boards and folders on the market some years ago. Since that time the number of Americans collecting coins has increased many-fold.

The Production of Coins

To collect coins intelligently it is necessary to have some knowledge of the manner in which our coins are produced. They are made in factories called "mints." The Mint of the United States was established at Philadelphia by a resolution of Congress dated April 2, 1792. The Act also provided for the coinage of gold eagles ($10), half-eagles and quarter-eagles, the silver dollar, half-dollar, quarter-dollar, dime (originally spelled "disme") and the half-disme or half-dime; the copper cent and half cent. According to the Treasury Department, the first coins struck were one-cent and half-cent pieces, in March of 1793 on a hand-operated press. Most numismatic authorities consider the half-disme of 1792 as the first United States coinage, quoting the words of George Washington as their authority, Washington, in his annual address, November 6, 1792, having said, "There has been a small beginning in the coining of the Half-Dimes, the want of small coins in circulation calling the first attention to them." In the new Philadelphia Mint are exhibited a number of implements, etc., from the original mint, and some coins discovered when the old building was wrecked. These coins included half-dismes, and the placard identifying them states that Washington furnished the silver and gave the coined pieces to his friends as souvenirs.

Prior to the adoption of the Constitution, the Continental Congress arranged for the issuance of copper coins under private contract. These are known as the "Fugio cents" from the design of the piece, which shows a sundial and the Latin word "fugio"—"I Fly" or, in connection with the sundial, "Time Flies." The ever appropriate motto. "Mind Your Business," is also on the coin.

In the manufacture of a given coin the first step is the cutting of the "die." Prior to the latter part of the nineteenth century dies for United States coins were "cut by hand." Briefly this method is as follows: The design having been determined, a drawing the exact size of the coin is made. A tracing is made from this drawing. A piece of steel is smoothed and coated with transfer wax, and the tracing impressed into the wax. The engraver then tools out the steel where the relief or raised effect is required. If the design is such that it can all be produced by cutting away steel, the die is hardened and ready for use. Some dies are not brought to a finished state, as some part of the design can perhaps be done better in relief. In that case, when all that can be accomplished to advantage in the die is completed, it is hardened, and a soft-steel impression is taken from it, and the unfinished parts are then completed. This piece of steel is in turn hardened and, by a press, driven into another piece of soft-steel, thus making a die which, when hardened, is ready for the making of coins.

This hand method of cutting dies accounts for the many die varieties of early United States coins. Where the amount of coinage of a given year was large enough to wear out several dies, each new die placed in the coining press created another die variety of that year. The dies being cut by hand, no two were exactly alike in every detail, even though some of the major elements (head, wreath, etc.) were sunk into the die by individual master punches. Of the cents dated 1794, over sixty different die varieties have been discovered.

Hundreds of dies are now used by the mints of the United States each year, but they are all made from one master die, which is produced in the following manner:

After the design is settled upon, the plaster of paris or wax model is prepared several times the actual size of the coin. When this model is finished an electrotype (an exact duplicate in metal) is made and prepared for the reducing lathe. The reducing lathe is a machine, working on the principle of the pantograph, only in this case the one point traces or follows the form of the model while another and much smaller point in the form of a drill cuts away the steel and produces a reduced size die of the model. The die is finished and details are sharpened or worked over by an engraver with chisel and graver. The master die is used to make duplicates in soft-steel which are then hardened and ready for the coining press. To harden dies, they are placed in cast-iron boxes packed with carbon to exclude the air, and when heated to a bright red are cooled suddenly with water.

In the coinage operations the first step is to prepare the metal. The alloys used are: silver coins, 90% silver and 10% copper; five-cent pieces, 75% copper and 25% nickel; one-cent pieces, 95% copper and 5% zinc. (The 1943 cent consists of steel coated with zinc; and the five-cent piece 1942-1945 contains 35% silver, 56% copper and 9% manganese.) Under the Coinage Act of 1965, the composition of dimes, quarters and half dollars was changed to eliminate or reduce the silver content of these coins. The copper-nickel "clad" dimes, quarters, halves and dollars are composed of an outer layer of copper-nickel (75% copper and 25% nickel) bonded to an inner core of pure copper. The silver clad half dollar and dollar have an outer layer of 80% silver bonded to an inner core of 21% silver, with a total content of 40% silver.

Alloys are melted in crucibles and poured into molds to form ingots. The ingots are in the form of thin bars and vary in size according to the denomination of the coin. The width is sufficient to allow three or more coins to be cut from the strips.

The ingots are next put through rolling mills to reduce the thickness to required limits. The strips are then fed into cutting presses which cut circular blanks (planchets) of the approximate size of the finished coin. The blanks are run through annealing furnaces to soften them; next through tumbling barrels, rotating cylinders containing cleaning solutions which clean and burnish the metal, and finally into centrifugal drying machines.

The blanks are next fed into a milling machine which produces the raised or upset rim. The blank is now ready for the coining press.

The blank is held firmly by a collar, as it is struck, under heavy pressure varying from 40 tons for the one-cent pieces and dimes to 170 tons for silver dollars. Upper and lower dies impress the design on both sides of the coin. The pressure is sufficient to produce a raised surface level with that of the milled rim. The collar holding the blank for silver or clad coins is grooved. The pressure forces the metal into the grooves of the collar, producing the "reeding" on the finished coin.

How a Proof Coin Is Made

Selected dies are inspected for perfection and are highly polished and cleaned. They are again wiped clean or polished after every 15 to 25 impressions and are replaced frequently to avoid imperfections from worn dies. Coinage blanks are polished and cleaned to assure high quality in striking. They are then hand fed into the coinage press one at a time, each blank receiving two blows from the dies to bring up sharp, high relief details. The coinage operation is done at slow speed with extra pressure. Finished proofs are individually inspected and are handled by gloves or tongs. They also receive a final inspection by packers before being sonically sealed in special plastic cases.

Certain coins, including Lincoln cents, Buffalo nickels, Quarter Eagles, Half Eagles, Eagles and Double Eagles, between the years 1908 and 1916 were made with a matte or sandblast surface. Matte proofs have a dull frosted surface which is produced by special treatment after striking.

Mints and Mint Marks

In addition to the Philadelphia Mint, the U.S. Government has from time to time established branch mints in various parts of the country. At the present time a branch mint operates in Denver. Starting in 1968, proof sets and some of the regular coins are produced at the San Francisco Assay Office. The Denver Mint has operated since 1906. A mint was operated at New Orleans from 1838 to 1861 and again from 1879 to 1909. Mints were also in service at Carson City, Nevada, from 1870 to 1893; at Charlotte, North Carolina, from 1838 to 1861; at Dahlonega, Georgia, from 1838 to 1861; and at San Francisco from 1854 to 1955.

Coins struck at Philadelphia (except 1942 to 1945 five-cent pieces) do not carry a mint mark. The mint mark is found only on coins struck at the branch mints. It is a small letter, usually found on the reverse side. The Lincoln cent is one exception to the rule. All coins minted after 1967 have the mint mark on the obverse. The letters to signify the various mints are as follows:

"C" for Charlotte, North Carolina (on gold coins only).

"CC" for Carson City, Nevada.

"D" for Dahlonega, Georgia (gold coins only, 1838 to 1861).

"D" for Denver, Colorado (from 1906 to date).

"O" for New Orleans, Louisiana.

"P" for Philadelphia, Pennsylvania.

"S" for San Francisco, California.

The mint mark is of utmost importance to collectors due to the fact that the coinage at the branch mints has usually been much smaller than at Philadelphia and many of the branch mint pieces are very scarce.

Location of Mint Marks

Half Cents — All coined at Philadelphia, no mint mark.

Large Cents — All coined at Philadelphia, no mint mark.

Flying Eagle Cents — All coined at Philadelphia, no mint mark.

Indian Cents — 1908 and 1909, under the wreath on reverse side.

Lincoln Cents — Under the date.

Two Cents, nickel Three Cents — All coined at Philadelphia, no mint mark.

Three Cents Silver — All coined at Philadelphia, except 1851 New Orleans mint — reverse side.

Shield Nickels — All coined at Philadelphia, no mint mark.

Liberty Nickels — All coined at Philadelphia except 1912 S and D — reverse side to left of word CENTS.

Buffalo Nickels — Reverse side under words FIVE CENTS.

Jefferson Nickels — Reverse side at right of the building. Starting 1968, on obverse near date.

Jefferson Five-Cent Pieces (silver, 1942-1945 inclusive) — Above dome on reverse.

Half Dimes — Reverse side either within or below the wreath.

Dimes — Old types on reverse side below or within wreath; Mercury type (1916-1945) on the reverse to left of the fasces. Roosevelt type starting 1946, at left of base of torch. Starting 1968, on obverse above date.

Twenty Cents — Reverse, under the eagle.

Quarter Dollars — Old types on reverse under eagle; Standing Liberty type (after 1916) obverse to left of date; Washington type on reverse under eagle Starting 1968, on obverse right of ribbon.

Half Dollars — 1838-1839 above date; 1840-1915 on reverse below eagle. 1916 and some 1917 on obverse below TRUST; other 1917-1947 on lower left reverse below branch. Franklin, above liberty bell beam. Kennedy, left of olive branch near claw. Starting 1968, on obverse beneath truncation.

Dollars — Old types, on reverse under eagle; Peace type on reverse near eagle's wing. Eisenhower type, above date. Anthony type, at left of shoulder.

Trade Dollars — On reverse under eagle.

Gold Dollars — Reverse under wreath.

Quarter Eagles ($2.50) — 1838 and 1839 over the date; other dates previous to 1907 on reverse under the eagle; Indian type (1908-29) on reverse lower left.

Three Dollar Pieces — Reverse under the wreath.

Half Eagles ($5.00) — Same as quarter eagles.

Eagles ($10.00) — Reverse under eagle; after 1907 at left of value.

Double Eagles ($20.00) — Old types on reverse under eagle; St. Gaudens (after 1907) above the date.

MINT MARKS

1908 and 1909 Indian Cents. San Francisco Mint only.

S or D found below date on obverse of Lincoln Cents.

Three-cent Silver, 1851 is only date this denomination produced at a branch mint. (New Orleans.)

MINT MARKS

Liberty Head Nickel 1912 S and D only, on reverse side.

Buffalo Nickel, on reverse side under "FIVE CENTS."

Jefferson Nickel, right of building 1938-42, 1946-64.

Jefferson 5c Silver 1942 to 1945. Above dome on reverse side.

Jefferson Nickel. Starting 1968, on obverse near date.

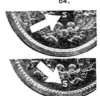

Half Dime. On reverse within, or below wreath.

Dime—old type. Reverse side. 1872-75-76 etc. Has mint mark within wreath also, as shown for half-dimes.

Barber Dime. Below wreath, reverse side.

Mercury Dime. On reverse to left of the fasces.

Roosevelt Dime 1946 to 1964

Roosevelt Dime. Starting 1968, on obverse above date.

Twenty-cent Piece. On reverse, under Eagle.

Quarter — old type. On reverse, under Eagle.

Barber Quarter. On reverse, under Eagle.

Standing Liberty Quarter. Very small mint mark found on obverse at left of date.

[7]

MINT MARKS

Washington Quarter, under eagle 1932-64.

Washington Quarter. Starting 1968, on obverse right of ribbon.

Half Dollar 1838-0 and 1839-0. On obverse, above date. (See page 66.)

Half Dollar, Barber and earlier types. On reverse, under Eagle.

Standing Liberty Half Dollar. 1916-1917 on obverse.

Standing Liberty Half Dollar. 1917 and later dates on reverse. (Either obverse or reverse on 1917.)

Franklin Half Dollar. Above liberty bell beam.

Kennedy Half Dollar, left of olive branch 1964 only.

Kennedy Half Dollar. Starting 1968, on obverse beneath truncation.

Silver Dollar—old types. On reverse, under Eagle.

Peace Type Dollar. On reverse, tip of eagle's wing.

Trade Dollar. On reverse, under Eagle.

Gold Dollar. On reverse, under wreath.

Quarter Eagle. 1838 and 1839 over date.

Quarter Eagle. On reverse under eagle until 1879.

MINT MARKS

Quarter Eagle—Indian Type. On reverse, lower left.

Three-Dollar Gold. On reverse under wreath.

Eagle—old types. On reverse, under eagle.

Half Eagles. Mint marks found in the same position as Quarter Eagles.

Eagle — After 1907. At left of value.

Double Eagle—old types. On reverse under Eagle.

Double Eagle — After 1907. Above date.

DISTINGUISHING MARKS

The illustrations and explanations in this section will help the collector to identify certain well-known varieties.

HALF CENTS OF 1795-1796 SHOWING LOCATION OF POLE TO CAP

The end of the staff or pole lies parallel with the line of the bust, which is pointed. The die-maker, probably through error, omitted the pole on some of the dies of 1795 and 1796.

Pole to Cap

No Pole to Cap

Stemless Wreath

Stems to Wreath

STEMLESS WREATH VARIETY OF HALF CENTS AND LARGE CENTS Observe the reverse side for this variety. Illustrations at left show both stemless and stems to wreath types for easy comparison—stemless wreath found on 1804, 1805, 1806, Half cents. 1797, 1802, 1803 Large cents.

1804 HALF CENT PROTRUDING TONGUE OR SPIKED CHIN VARIETY

DISTINGUISHING MARKS

Plain 4

Crosslet 4

Details showing differences in 1804 plain 4 and crosslet 4. Note serif on horizontal bar of figure 4 as shown at right.

THE 1856 FLYING EAGLE CENT

Collectors are advised to inspect any 1856 Flying Eagle cent carefully.

A few tests will aid in establishing genuineness of this cent, as follows:

THE DATE

The 6 in the date should be as illustrated. If the lower half is thick, it is probably an altered 1858. A magnifying glass will often reveal poor workmanship.

The figure 5 slants slightly to the right on a genuine 1856. The vertical bar points to the center of the ball just beneath. On the 1858, this bar points *outside* the ball. (Compare the two illustrations.)

THE LEGEND

The center of the O in OF is crude and almost squared on the genuine 1856, but on the large letter 1858 it is rounded.

The letters A and M in America are joined in both the 1856 and large letter 1858, but they join at a slight angle on the 1856, while the bottom of the letters form a smooth curve on the 1858 large letter cent.

Large Letters

Small Letters

1858 FLYING EAGLE CENT

Letters A and M in the word AMERICA are joined on the LARGE LETTER variety. They are separated on the SMALL LETTER variety.

DISTINGUISHING MARKS

1864 BRONZE INDIAN HEAD CENT WITH "L" ON RIBBON

A small "L," the initial of the designer Longacre, was added to the Indian design late in 1864 and was continued through 1909. For coins in less than fine condition, this small letter will often be worn away. The point of the bust is rounded on the 1864 variety without "L"; pointed on the variety with "L." The initial must be visible, however, for the 1864 variety to bring the higher premium. If the coin is turned slightly so that the Indian faces the observer, the highlighted details will usually appear to better advantage.

Small Motto

Large Motto

TWO CENTS OF 1864

Details explain the differences in these two well-known varieties. On the obverse, D in God is narrow on the large motto. The stem to the leaf shows plainly on the small motto variety. There is no stem on the large motto coin. First T in TRUST, small motto variety, is closer to ribbon crease at left.

(At top) 1909 Initials appear on reverse. (At right) Initials appear beneath shoulder, 1918 and later.

LINCOLN CENTS SHOWING LOCATION OF INITIALS V D B

1918-S QUARTER 8 OVER 7

A variety of this kind is rarely found in coinage of the twentieth century.

[11]

DISTINGUISHING MARKS

1938D over S Nickel Variety

1955 Cent Error
"Doubled Die" Obverse

Large Date Cent
1960

Small Date Cent
1960

1942 Dime
with 2 over 1

CONDITION OF COINS

FAIR — Coin has sufficient design and letters to be easily identified. Excessive wear.

GOOD or G. — All of design, every feature and legend must be plain and date clear.

VERY GOOD or V. GOOD or V.G. — Features all clear and bold. Better than good, but not quite fine.

FINE or F. — Obviously a circulated coin but little wear. Mint luster gone. All letters in LIBERTY and mottoes clear.

VERY FINE or V. FINE or V.F. — Shows enough wear on high spots to be noticeable. Still retains enough detail to be desirable.

EXTREMELY FINE or E. FINE or E.F. — Slightly circulated with some luster but faint evidence of wear.

ABOUT UNCIRCULATED or A.U. — Has nearly full uncirculated luster, but shows light signs of handling.

UNCIRCULATED or UNC. — New. Regular mint striking, but never placed in circulation. Older pieces may be tarnished or "toned."

PROOF or PF. — Coins with mirrorlike surface, specially struck for coin collectors. Also sandblast and matte proof. See page 5.
Pre-1968 branch mint coins having a mirrorlike surface are not proofs but are first strikings of new dies.

IMPORTANT: Damaged coins, such as those which are bent, corroded, scratched, holed, nicked, stained, oxidized, or mutilated, are worth less than those without defects. *Flawless uncirculated coins are generally worth more than values quoted in this book.* Coins which have been cleaned to simulate uncirculated luster are worth considerably less than perfect pieces.

Brief guides to grading are placed before each major coin type in this book. For those readers who desire more detailed descriptions of all coin grades, we recommend OFFICIAL A.N.A. GRADING STANDARDS FOR UNITED STATES COINS, by The American Numismatic Association.

Preserving and Cleaning Coins

Most numismatists will tell you to "never clean a coin" and it is good advice; however, every collector tries to clean a coin sooner or later, so we are passing on a few tips here.

In the first place some effort should be made to keep uncirculated and proof coins bright so they won't need cleaning. Tarnish on a coin is purely a chemical process caused by oxygen in the air acting on the metal or by chemicals with which the coin comes in contact. One of the commonest chemicals causing tarnish is sulphur; most paper, with the exception of specially manufactured "sulphur-free" kinds, contains sulphur due to the sulphuric acid that is used in paper manufacture. Therefore do not wrap coins in ordinary paper; also keep uncirculated and proof coins away from rubber bands (a rubber band placed on a silver coin for a few days will produce a black stripe on the coin where the band touched).

The utmost in protection is received by wrapping the coin in lead or aluminum foil and then storing it in an airtight box.

Many coins become marred by careless handling. Always hold the coin by the edge. The accompanying illustration shows the right and wrong way to handle numismatic specimens. It is a breach of numismatic etiquette to handle another collector's coin except by the edge, even if it is not an uncirculated or proof piece.

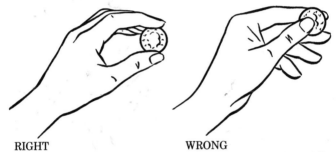

RIGHT   WRONG

If you must satisfy the urge to try to clean coins, experiment first with some ordinary coins.

Modern silver coins can often be cleaned with a paste consisting of baking soda and water without harming the coin. Hold about a teaspoonful of paste in the palm of one hand. Work the coin gently into the paste with the other hand. Rinse the coin in clear water and dry with a clean blotter. DO NOT use kitchen cleanser, silver polish, a pencil eraser or other abrasives on any coins.

Copper and bronze coins are very difficult to clean. Scrubbing with an abrasive makes the high parts of the coin bright while the other parts will look dirtier than ever, giving the piece a very unnatural appearance that considerably lessens its value in the numismatic market. The use of acids and buffing wheels also produces an unnatural appearance.

No amount of scrubbing or cleaning, or the use of acids or buffers, will restore the original mint lustre to a coin.

Starting a Collection

One may start a collection of United States coins with very little expense by systematically assembling the various dates and mint marks of all the types and denominations that are now in general circulation. Whitman's coin folders make this possible.

With the exception of the price paid for the coin folder, collecting coins received in everyday business transactions entails no expense whatever; a Jefferson nickel taken out of circulation, for example, can always be spent for 5 cents if the occasion arrives. Filling a board or two out of circulation is probably the best method of determining whether coin collecting appeals to you. Not everyone can be a successful coin collector. It requires patience, intelligence of a high order, and a certain desire to know the meaning behind a lot of things that at first glance and to the ordinary mortal appear meaningless. You may not be cut out to be a collector but you'll never know until you look further into the subject, and if by the time a board or two of coins are collected you have no burning desire to acquire many more different coins, you will probably never be a collector. However, the chances are that you will be, because if you have read this far in this book it shows that you are interested in the subject.

Although forming a collection "out-of-circulation" is the least expensive method, it is possible not only to have a lot of fun with such a collection but also to profit to a certain degree. The cheapest coins to collect are the current Lincoln head cents. Many dates can be found in circulation. There are scores of coins in circulation dated after 1930 that are worth a premium to collectors. It is possible to collect hundreds of different United States coins out of general circulation.

Perfection is the goal of every endeavor and coin collecting is no exception. After a board has been filled with circulated specimens the next step will be to replace pieces with coins in uncirculated condition; or perhaps to start collecting the obsolete series; in either case it will be necessary to purchase some coins from dealers or other collectors. The most logical way to keep abreast with the market, or obtain the addresses of the country's leading dealers, is to subscribe to one or more of the trade publications (see page 3 for list of the coin magazines). These magazines carry advertisements of various dealers listing coins for sale. Moreover, through this source the beginner may obtain price lists and catalogs from the dealers.

There are several good reference books available at reasonable prices which will be helpful to the collector who wishes to know more about U. S. coins and paper money. The GUIDE BOOK OF U. S. COINS (Red Book) is an expanded version of THE HANDBOOK. It lists retail values of all regular U. S. coins and also lists all coins of the U. S. Colonial period and private and territorial gold coins.

Most coin, book and hobby dealers can supply the following titles:

Guide Book of U.S. Coins — Yeoman
U.S. Commemorative Coinage — Slabaugh
Let's Collect Coins — Bressett
U.S. Pattern, Experimental & Trial Pieces — Judd
Patriotic Civil War Tokens — Fuld
Guide to Civil War Store Cards — Fuld
The Fantastic 1804 Dollar — Newman & Bressett
Guide Book of Modern U.S. Currency — Shafer
U.S. Fractional Currency — Rothert
Buying and Selling U.S. Coins — Bressett
Official Grading Standards for U.S. Coins — A.N.A.

JOIN A COIN CLUB

A beginner should join a "coin club" if he is fortunate enough to live in a city which has one. The association with more experienced collectors will be of great benefit. Practically all the larger cities have one or more clubs and they are being rapidly organized in the smaller towns. The publications mentioned on page 3 carry lists of coin clubs and special events such as coin shows and conventions.

Abbreviations

Like most businesses the coin trade has developed a number of abbreviations which are used generally in magazine advertising to conserve space in listing coins. To many a beginner, reading such an advertisement for the first time, it is difficult to understand. However, the abbreviations are not numerous and they can be quickly mastered. Some of the abbreviations are peculiar to particular types or denominations and are mentioned in this book in their respective places. The more general abbreviations are:

Obv. or Ob. — Obverse. The "heads" side of a coin.

Rev., Rx., or R. — Reverse. The "tails" side of a coin.

Var., Vars. — Variety, Varieties.

Ty. or T. — Type. (A frequent abbreviation is N.T. or O.T., meaning new type or old type.)

Lib. — Liberty.

Lge. or Lg. — Large.

Sm. — Small.

The condition of the coin is the most frequently abbreviated item. The common condition abbreviations are:

Pr. or Pf. — Proof.

Unc., Uncir., or U. — Uncirculated.

E.F., X.F., or Ex.F. — Extremely Fine. (Also Extra Fine.)

V.F. — Very Fine. (The "V" is sometimes used to denote "very" in other cases, such as very rare, very scarce.)

V.G. or V.Gd. — Very Good.

G. or Gd. — Good.

Fr. — Fair.

Brill., or Bril. — Brilliant.

An example of an abbreviated coin listing is as follows:

Standing Liberty Quarters

1917-S Var. 2, VG, Sc. \$0.00

The figures "1917" stand for the year of coinage, "S" for the San Francisco mint mark, "Var. 2" means the piece is of the second variety, "VG" is the condition, "Sc." meaning the piece is scarce. The price which follows is the value of the coin.

UNITED STATES PAPER MONEY

Paper money issued by the United States government is collected widely in this country. The first issue of "greenbacks" was made in 1861; paper money was not issued by our government for circulation prior to that date. Collectors of U.S. notes prefer them in crisp, new condition; therefore the old style large-sized notes in worn condition are usually worth very little more than face value.

Before the issuance of the first U.S. government paper money, many banks throughout the country issued their own currency. These issues are commonly referred to as "broken bank notes" although that is somewhat of a misnomer as many of the banks did not "go broke" (a few are still in existence) and redeemed their paper money issues. There are thousands of varieties of these notes in existence, most of which are very common and worth from 25¢ to 50¢ each. Before and during the American Revolution the various individual states and the Continental Congress issued paper money. The commoner varieties of these Colonial notes are worth from \$2.00 to \$5.00; a few are quite rare.

U. S. HALF CENTS
Issued from 1793 through 1857
Metal: Copper.

All half cents are really scarce, but the series has never enjoyed the popularity of some of the other series, hence the more common dates of half cents are not extremely valuable.

The series does, however, contain a number of rarities, 1796 being the rarest date. The dates 1840, 1841, 1842, 1843, 1844, 1845, 1846, 1847, 1848, 1849 small date, and 1852 were issued in proof only, and in two varieties. Those with the ten large berries and one small berry on the reverse are called the "originals" and those with eleven small berries on the reverse are termed "restrikes." A restrike is an impression made from genuine dies but at a later time than the date shown on the coin.

Terms used in describing Half Cents:

Lettered Edge (*1793, 1794, 1795, and 1797*) — The words "Two Hundred for a Dollar" are found on the edge of some or all varieties of these dates.

Pole to Cap (*or no pole to cap*) — All varieties of the 1794 have a "pole to cap," that is, the pole shows beside the head of Liberty. The years 1795 and 1796 are found with the pole and also "without" a pole.

Stemless Wreath; Stems to Wreath (1804, 1805, and 1806.) — On some of the reverses of these dates the wreath has stems; on others the wreath does not have stems. (See page 9.)

Crosslet 4; Plain 4 — On those of 1804 only. The "4" in the date appears on some varieties with a serif; that is known as the "crosslet 4." The variety without serif is known as the "plain 4." There is also a variety of the 1804 known as the "spiked chin" or "protruding tongue" on which Liberty appears to be sticking out her tongue. (See page 9.)

Overdates — An overdate is the result of using a die of a previous year and re-cutting the new date over the old figures. In the half cent series, the following overdates are found: 1802 over 1800; 1808 over 7; 1809 over 6. A variety of 1797 has a "1 over 1" which is actually not an overdate but an error in die cutting — the engraver rather than cut a new die merely cut another figure 1.

The following abbreviations are found in numismatic literature referring to half cents.

Ed. – edge	*Let.* – lettered	*Perf.* – perfect	*Sm.* – small
Lg. – large	*Ov.* – over	*Pl.* – plain	

LIBERTY CAP TYPE 1793-1797

FAIR—*Clear enough to identify.*
GOOD—*Outline of bust clear, no details. Date readable. Reverse lettering incomplete.*
VERY GOOD—*Some hair details. Reverse lettering complete.*
FINE—*Most of hair detail shows.*

	Quan. Minted	Fair	Good	V. Good	Fine
1793	35,334	$200.00	$400.00	$500.00	$825.00

[16]

HALF CENTS

Head facing
right
1794-1797

	Quan. Minted	Fair	Good	V. Good	Fine
1794	81,600	$45.00	$65.00	$110.00	$185.00
1795	134,600	42.50	62.50	100.00	175.00
1796 Pole to cap	5,090	450.00	900.00	1,500	2,750
No pole to cap	1,390	650.00	1,800	2,750	4,500
1797 Lettered edge	} 119,215	100.00	200.00	310.00	550.00
Plain edge		35.00	60.00	85.00	140.00

DRAPED BUST TYPE 1800-1808

FAIR—*Clear enough to identify.*

GOOD—*Bust outline clear, few details, date readable. Reverse lettering worn and incomplete.*

VERY GOOD—*Some drapery shows. Date and legends complete.*

FINE—*Shoulder drapery and hair over brow worn smooth.*

1800	211,530	7.00	15.00	17.50	26.00
1802	14,366	45.00	85.00	130.00	230.00
1803	97,900	6.50	15.00	17.50	26.00
1804	1,055,312	6.50	15.00	17.50	26.00
1805	814,464	6.50	15.00	17.50	26.00
1806	356,000	6.50	15.00	17.50	26.00
1807	476,000	6.50	15.00	17.50	26.00
1808 8 over 7	} 400,000	18.00	30.00	50.00	85.00
Normal date		6.50	15.00	17.50	26.00

CLASSIC HEAD TYPE 1809-1836

GOOD—*LIBERTY only partly visible on hair band. Lettering, date, stars, worn but visible.*

VERY GOOD—*LIBERTY entirely visible on hair band. Lower curls worn.*

FINE—*Only part wear on LIBERTY and hair at top worn in spots.*

1809 9 over 6	} 1,154,572	6.50	15.00	17.50	26.00
Normal date		6.00	14.00	16.00	24.00

HALF CENTS

	Quan. Minted	Good	V. Good	Fine	Proof
1810	215,000	$14.00	$19.00	$33.00	
1811	63,140	30.00	45.00	80.00	
1825	63,000	14.00	17.00	22.00	
1826	234,000	14.00	16.00	20.00	
1828	606,000	14.00	16.00	20.00	
1829	487,000	14.00	16.00	20.00	
1831 Original (Large berries on wreath)	2,200				$1,650
Restrike (Small berries on wreath)					1,250
1832	*estimated 154,000	14.00	16.00	20.00	
1833	*estimated 120,000	14.00	16.00	20.00	
1834	*estimated 141,000	14.00	16.00	20.00	
1835	*estimated 398,000	14.00	16.00	20.00	
1836 Original (Large berries on wreath)					1,250
Restrike (Small berries on wreath)					——

*The figures given here are thought to be correct, although official mint records give the same quantities for 1833-36 rather than 1832-35.

No half cents were struck in 1837. Because of the great need for small change, however, a large number of tokens similar in size to current half cents and large cents were issued privately by businessmen who needed them in commerce. One of the most popular pieces is listed and illustrated below.

1837 Token	15.00	20.00	30.00

BRAIDED HAIR TYPE 1840-1857

1840 Original (Large berries on wreath)	800.00
Restrike (Small berries on wreath)	800.00
1841 Original (Large berries)	850.00
Restrike (Small berries)	800.00
1842 Original (Large berries)	800.00
Restrike (Small berries)	800.00

HALF CENTS

Proof*
1843 Original (Large berries) $800.00
    Restrike (Small berries) 800.00
1844 Original (Large berries) 800.00
    Restrike (Small berries) 800.00
1845 Original (Large berries) 800.00
    Restrike (Small berries) 800.00
1846 Original (Large berries) 800.00
    Restrike (Small berries) 800.00
1847 Original (Large berries) 800.00
    Restrike (Small berries) 800.00
1848 Original (Large berries) 800.00
    Restrike (Small berries) 800.00
1849 Small date, original (Large berries) 900.00
    Small date, restrike (Small berries)................................. 900.00

VERY GOOD—*Beads uniformly distinct. Hairlines show in spots.*
FINE—*Hairlines above ear worn. Beads sharp.*
VERY FINE—*Lowest curl shows wear, hair otherwise distinct.*

	Quan. Minted	Good	V. Good	Fine	V. Fine
1849 Large date	39,864	$14.00	$18.00	$22.00	$34.00
1850	39,812	14.00	18.00	22.00	34.00
1851	147,672	13.00	17.00	20.00	27.50

Proof
1852 Original (Large berries) .... ——
    Restrike (Small berries) 825.00

	Good	V. Good	Fine	V. Fine
1853 129,694	13.00	17.00	20.00	27.50
1854 55,358	13.00	17.00	20.00	27.50
1855 56,500	13.00	17.00	20.00	27.50
1856 40,430	14.00	18.00	22.00	32.00
857 35,180	14.00	18.00	28.00	35.00

U.S. LARGE COPPER CENTS
Issued from 1793 through 1857

A very interesting and popular series; more has been written about these coins than any other United States series. They were coined in every year during the period 1793 to 1857 except 1815. There are 60 different die varieties of the cents of 1794 and most of the other dates have a dozen or more. These variations are sometimes slight, often being merely the position of a leaf in the wreath or the spacing of the figures of the date.

In advertisements listing large cents, it is not uncommon to read such notations as, "1807 S. 273" or "D. 203." These refer to die varieties; "S" denoting Sheldon, "D" for Doughty. Various numismatic students have made a study of the varieties of various years and the varieties are named after these students; Crosby for 1793, Chapman for 1794, Doughty for 1795, 1797 to 1814 inclusive, Clapp for 1798; Newcomb 1801, 1802 and 1803, Sheldon for 1793-1814, and Newcomb for the years 1816 to 1857 inclusive. However, most collectors are content to acquire just one of each date, and leave the collecting of die varieties to the specialist.

Recommended Reference Books

For those who care to go into the detail study of large cent varieties the following books are recommended:

"Penny Whimsy" by Sheldon, Paschal and Breen (1793-1814).

"The Cents and Half Cents of 1793" by S. S. Crosby.

"The Cents of 1794" by S. H. Chapman.

"United States Cents" by Francis W. Doughty.

"Cents of 1798 and 1799" by Geo. Clapp.

"Cents of 1801, 1802 and 1803" by Newcomb.

"United States Copper Cents 1816-1857" by Newcomb.

"Cents 1795, 1796, 1797 and 1800" by Clapp.

Condition Is Important

Condition plays a big part in the value of a large cent, especially the early dates. Evidence of this is brought out by a comparison of the lowest grade price with the highest in the premium values following.

Rare Dates Often Faked

In collecting large cents these three dates especially should be purchased from reliable dealers only who will guarantee the genuineness of the coins. The 1793 is frequently "electrotyped." An electrotype can generally be determined by examining the edge to determine if two shells have been placed together. Cents of 1799 will be found "electrotyped" and also made by altering the "8" of the more common 1798 to a "9." An examination of a suspicious piece under a magnifying glass will generally reveal the alteration. Fake cents of 1804 are made by altering most any of the other dates of the same general type, an 1801 being most frequently used. A quick way to check this point is to determine whether the "O" in the date is directly opposite the "O" in OF on the reverse. The peculiarity is found on genuine cents of 1804 and if the piece has been made by altering another date the cipher and the O will not be exactly opposite.

LARGE CENTS

Restrike of the 1804 Cent

A fake 1804 was manufactured about the year 1860 to satisfy the demand for this rare date. This piece was known as the "restrike" but fortunately for collectors it was a patchwork job and easily distinguished from a genuine 1804 cent. An old rusty die was used for the obverse which makes the field of the coin pitted and a die of the year 1820, which is much different from an 1804, was used for the reverse. To aid collectors, an illustration of the 1804 restrike is shown here. This piece is not a true restrike, and was not made at the mint.

Terms Used in Describing Large Cents

Chain Type — The first type of year 1793, has an endless chain of links on the reverse.

Lettered Edge — Some 1793, 1974 and 1795 cents have lettering, "One Hundred for a Dollar" on the edge.

Broken Die — Cracks or lumps on coin caused by the die breaking or cracking.

Stemless Wreath — See Half Cents.

Wreaths to Stems — See Half Cents.

Crosslet and Plain 4 — See Half Cents.

Overdate — See Half Cents.

The terms, "wide date," "compact date," "large letters," "small letters," "plain hair cord," "beaded hair cord," "large fraction," "small fraction," etc., are also used and are self-explanatory.

The following abbreviations are used in describing large cents:

Frac. – fraction	*Lib.* – liberty	*Pl. Ed.* – plain edge	*Up.* – upright
Lg. large	*Ov.* – over	*Sl.* – slanting	
Let. Ed. – lettered edge	*Perf.* – perfect	*Sm.* – small	

FLOWING HAIR, CHAIN TYPE REVERSE 1793

FAIR—*Date and devices clear enough to identify.*

GOOD—*Lettering worn but readable. Bust has no detail.*

VERY GOOD—*Date and lettering distinct, some details of head visible.*

FINE—*About half of hair, etc. details show.*

	Quan. Minted	Fair	Good	V. Good	Fine
1793 AMERI. in legend	⎱ 36,103	$225.00	$550.00	$800.00	$1,500
AMERICA	⎰	200.00	450.00	675.00	1,300

[21]

LARGE CENTS
FLOWING HAIR, WREATH TYPE REVERSE 1793

Strawberry Sprig Variety→

	Quan. Minted	Fair	Good	V. Good	Fine
1793 Wreath type....................	63,353	$175.00	$325.00	$475.00	$775.00
1793 Strawberry sprig var. (4 known)			——		

LIBERTY CAP TYPE 1793-1796

1793 Liberty Cap	11,056	250.00	400.00	750.00	1,250
1794	918,521	17.00	32.00	55.00	110.00
1795 Plain edge...................	501,500	17.00	32.00	55.00	110.00
Lettered edge.................	37,000	20.00	40.00	75.00	130.00
1796 Liberty Cap	109,825	20.00	40.00	75.00	130.00

DRAPED BUST TYPE 1796-1807

FAIR—*Clear enough to identify.*

GOOD—*Lettering worn, but clear; date clear. Bust lacks details.*

V. GOOD—*Drapery partly visible. Less wear in date and lettering.*

FINE—*Hair over brow is smooth, some detail showing in other parts of hair.*

1796 Draped Bust..................	363,375	17.00	32.00	55.00	110.00
1797 Normal wreath .... }	1,841,745	12.00	16.00	28.00	50.00
Stemless wreath .... }		18.00	35.00	60.00	115.00
1798 8 over 7................... }	897,510	17.00	25.00	50.00	90.00
Normal date.............. }		10.00	15.00	22.00	40.00
1799 (Beware of altered date)					
9 over 8................... }	42,540		325.00	550.00	1,000
Normal date.............. }			300.00	500.00	950.00
1800	2,822,175	9.00	14.00	19.00	32.00
1801	1,362,837	9.00	14.00	19.00	32.00
1802	3,435,100	8.00	12.00	17.00	30.00

LARGE CENTS

	Quan. Minted	Fair	Good	V. Good	Fine
1803	3,131,691	$8.00	$12.00	$17.00	$30.00
1804 Original	96,500	100.00	200.00	300.00	500.00
So-called "Mint Restrike" (See page 21)					
1805	941,166	8.00	12.00	17.00	30.00
1806	348,000	12.00	21.00	30.00	55.00
1807 7 over 6	} 829,221	8.00	12.00	17.00	35.00
Normal date		8.00	12.00	17.00	35.00

CLASSIC HEAD TYPE 1808-1814

FAIR—*Details clear enough to identify.*
GOOD—*Legends, stars, date worn, but plain.*
V. GOOD—*LIBERTY all readable. Ear shows. Details worn but plain.*
FINE—*Hair on forehead and before ear nearly smooth. Ear and hair under ear sharp.*

	Quan. Minted	Fair	Good	V. Good	Fine
1808	1,109,000	11.00	18.00	25.00	47.50
1809	222,867	25.00	50.00	80.00	150.00
1810	1,458,500	9.00	13.00	21.00	37.50
1811	218,025	19.00	34.00	55.00	120.00
1812	1,075,500	9.00	13.00	21.00	37.50
1813	418,000	12.00	21.00	30.00	65.00
1814	357,830	9.00	13.00	21.00	35.00

CORONET TYPE 1816-1857

GOOD—*Head details partly visible. Even wear in date and legends.*
V. GOOD—*LIBERTY, date, stars, legends clear. Part of hair cord visible.*
FINE—*All hairlines show. Hair cords show uniformly.*

	Quan. Minted	Good	V. Good	Fine
1816	2,820,982	4.50	6.00	10.00
1817	3,948,400	4.00	5.00	8.00
1818	3,167,000	4.00	5.00	8.00
1819	2,671,000	4.00	5.00	8.00
1820	4,407,550	4.00	5.00	8.00
1821	389,000	8.50	16.00	30.00
1822	2,072,339	4.50	6.00	9.00
1823	68,061	16.00	27.00	52.50
1824	1,193,939	4.50	6.00	11.00
1825	1,461,100	4.00	5.50	9.50
1826	1,517,425	4.00	5.50	9.50
1827	2,357,732	4.00	5.50	8.00
1828	2,260,624	4.00	5.00	7.00
1829	1,414,500	4.00	5.00	7.00
1830	1,711,500	4.00	5.00	7.00

LARGE CENTS

	Quan. Minted	Good	V. Good	Fine
1831	3,359,260	$3.75	$4.50	$6.00
1832	2,362,000	3.75	4.50	6.00
1833	2,739,000	3.75	4.50	6.00
1834	1,855,100	4.00	5.25	7.00
1835	3,878,400	3.75	4.50	6.50
1836	2,111,000	3.75	4.50	6.50
1837	5,558,300	3.75	4.50	6.00
1838	6,370,200	3.75	4.50	6.00
1839 9 over 6	} 3,128,661	55.00	80.00	165.00
Normal date		5.00	7.00	14.00

1840	2,462,700	3.75	4.50	6.00
1841	1,597,367	3.75	4.50	6.00
1842	2,383,390	3.75	4.50	6.00
1843	2,425,342	3.75	4.50	6.00
1844	2,398,752	3.75	4.50	6.00
1845	3,894,804	3.50	4.25	5.25
1846	4,120,800	3.50	4.25	5.25
1847	6,183,669	3.50	4.25	5.25
1848	6,415,799	3.50	4.25	5.25
1849	4,178,500	3.50	4.25	5.25
1850	4,426,844	3.50	4.25	5.25
1851	9,889,707	3.50	4.00	5.00
1852	5,063,094	3.50	4.00	5.00
1853	6,641,131	3.50	4.00	5.00
1854	4,236,156	3.50	4.00	5.00
1855	1,574,829	3.75	4.50	5.25
1856	2,690,463	3.75	4.50	5.25
1857	333,456	15.00	20.00	30.00

Only a small fraction of the Large Cents issued over a period of 64 years are available. It is an interesting fact that the Treasury Department made a special effort to retire these coins in 1857. They were considered too large for use in business transactions. The smaller coin was considerably more popular. Details of exchange are covered in a circular issued by the mint April 27, 1857.

Following are excerpts from this regulation:

"1. On and after the twenty-fifth day of May next, applications may be made at the mint for cents of the new issue in exchange for ... the Spanish Pillar Dollar, and the Mexican Dollar ... or in exchange for the copper cents heretofore issued.

2. The silver or copper coins must be in even sums of five dollars ... not exceeding fifty dollars. ... "

This bulletin will help us to understand what has become of a great many large copper cents.

SMALL CENTS
Authorized for Circulation in 1857

FLYING EAGLE TYPE 1856-1858

This coin was the first issue of the small cent. Those of 1856 are generally considered to be patterns but were issued in rather large number for a pattern coin. It is said that there were about 1,000 pieces struck of the commonest variety of the 1856 (copper-nickel or thick planchet, tobacco wreath on reverse). In all there are twelve varieties of the 1856. Cents of the flying eagle type dated 1857 and 1858 are common, except in proof condition; in that condition they are quite expensive. "United States of America" on the flying eagle cent of 1858 comes to two sizes of letters. These types are known as "small letters" and "large letters" (abbreviated S.L. and L.L.). On the small letter variety the A and M in America are separated; the large letter variety shows these two letters joined at the base.

Fake 1856's are made by altering an 1858. Such pieces are recognized by the thickness of the lower half of the manufactured "6." (See page 10.)

GOOD—*All details worn, but readable.*

V. GOOD—*Feather details and eye of Eagle are evident, but worn.*

FINE—*Eagle head details and feather tips sharp.*

V. FINE—*Eagle's eye very bold. Feather ends on right wing worn smooth, considerable detail in right wing and tail.*

EX. FINE—*All feathers in wing and tail plain. Eagle's breast will show some wear.*

Quan. Minted	Good	V. Good	Fine	V. Fine	Ex. Fine	Proof
1856	$550.00	$675.00	$800.00	$950.00	$1,100	$1,750
1857 17,450,000	4.50	5.50	7.50	15.00	40.00	
1858 All Kinds						
.... 24,600,000						
Large Letters.....	4.50	5.50	8.00	16.00	42.00	
Small Letters.....	4.50	5.50	8.00	16.00	42.00	

INDIAN HEAD TYPE 1859-1909

Those of the years 1859 to 1863 were struck in copper-nickel and are commonly termed "white cents" because the metal is of lighter color. In 1864 the metal was changed to the present-used bronze, although copper-nickel cents of 1864 were struck, too. Soon after the change of metal the initial "L," for the engraver Longacre, was placed on the ribbon of the headdress. The "L" variety was struck in smaller quantity than the earlier variety without it, and is therefore quite rare. The "L" appears on the ribbon under the last feather of the headdress on *all* other dates from 1865 to 1909. (See page 11.)

Abbreviations peculiar to this series are:

IH. or *IND. HD.* — Indian Head.

C-N or *Cop-Nic.* — Copper-nickel.

Note: Indian head cents having the date 1858 were not struck for circulation. They are patterns.

SMALL CENTS
Variety 1 — Copper-nickel, laurel wreath reverse 1859

GOOD—*No LIBERTY visible.*
V. GOOD—*At least three letters of LIBERTY readable.*
FINE—*LIBERTY completely visible.*
V. FINE—*Slight but even wear on LIBERTY.*

Without shield at top of
wreath on reverse

	Quan. Minted	Good	V. Good	Fine	V. Fine
1859 Indian Head...............	36,400,000	$2.25	$2.75	$6.00	$12.00

Variety 2 — Copper-nickel, oak wreath with shield 1860-1864

With shield
on reverse

1860	20,566,000	2.00	2.70	4.25	7.25
1861	10,100,000	4.00	5.50	10.00	14.00
1862	28,075,000	1.75	2.00	3.25	5.50
1863	49,840,000	1.75	2.00	3.25	5.50
1864 Cop.-Nic..................	13,740,000	3.00	4.00	6.25	9.50

Variety 3 — Bronze 1864-1909

1864 Bronze (no L on ribbon)... ⎱	39,233,714	1.50	2.25	4.00	9.00
1864 with L (see p. 11) .... ⎰		12.00	17.00	31.00	47.50
1865	35,429,286	1.50	2.25	4.00	7.50
1866	9,826,500	9.00	12.00	18.00	30.00
1867	9,821,000	9.00	12.00	18.00	30.00
1868	10,266,500	9.00	12.00	18.00	30.00
1869	6,420,000	15.00	20.00	40.00	60.00
1870	5,275,000	12.00	17.00	37.00	50.00
1871	3,929,500	15.00	21.00	40.00	55.00
1872	4,042,000	20.00	25.00	50.00	70.00
1873	11,676,500	4.00	5.50	11.00	17.50
1874	14,187,500	4.00	5.50	11.00	17.50
1875	13,528,000	4.00	5.50	11.00	17.50
1876	7,944,000	6.00	8.00	15.00	22.00
1877	852,500	100.00	125.00	180.00	225.00
1878	5,799,850	6.00	8.00	16.00	25.00
1879	16,231,200	1.15	1.75	3.50	7.00
1880	38,964,955	.70	.90	1.75	3.00
1881	39,211,575	.70	.90	1.75	3.00
1882	38,581,100	.70	.90	1.75	3.00
1883	45,598,109	.70	.90	1.75	3.00

SMALL CENTS

	Quan. Minted	Good	V. Good	Fine	V. Fine
1884	23,261,742	$ .85	$1.40	$3.00	$5.00
1885	11,765,384	1.75	3.00	4.75	9.00
1886	17,654,290	.85	1.50	3.25	5.50
1887	45,226,483	.50	.60	.90	1.70
1888	37,494,414	.50	.60	.90	1.70
1889	48,869,361	.50	.60	.90	1.70
1890	57,182,854	.50	.60	.90	1.70
1891	47,072,350	.50	.60	.90	1.70
1892	37,649,832	.50	.60	.90	1.70
1893	46,642,195	.50	.60	.90	1.70
1894	16,752,132	.75	1.35	3.00	5.00
1895	38,343,636	.40	.50	.75	1.50
1896	39,057,293	.40	.50	.75	1.50
1897	50,466,330	.40	.50	.75	1.50
1898	49,823,079	.40	.50	.75	1.50
1899	53,600,031	.40	.50	.75	1.50
1900	66,833,764	.35	.40	.60	1.10
1901	79,611,143	.35	.40	.60	1.10
1902	87,376,722	.35	.40	.60	1.10
1903	85,094,493	.35	.40	.60	1.10
1904	61,328,015	.35	.40	.60	1.10
1905	80,719,163	.35	.40	.60	1.10
1906	96,022,255	.35	.40	.60	1.10
1907	108,138,618	.35	.40	.60	1.10
1908	32,327,987	.35	.40	.60	1.10
1908S	1,115,000	12.00	13.00	15.00	23.00
1909 Indian	14,370,645	.50	.65	1.00	1.50
1909S Indian	309,000	50.00	57.50	67.50	82.50

LINCOLN TYPE, WHEAT EARS REVERSE
1909-1958

Variety 1 — Bronze 1909-1942

The first year of the Lincoln cent, 1909, comes with or without the small letters "VDB" on the reverse near the lower edge. These letters are the initials of the designer, Victor D. Brenner. There was some protest about the placing of the initials on the coin and they were removed, only to be replaced on the cents of 1918 and thereafter in new position, under Lincoln's bust, in letters so small that an uncirculated piece is often necessary for examination to find it.

GOOD—*Date worn but apparent. Lines in wheat ears missing.*
V. GOOD—*Lines show in upper wheat ears.*
FINE—*Wheat lines worn but visible.*
V. FINE—*Cheek and jaw bones worn but separated. No worn spots on wheat ears.*
EXTREMELY FINE—*Slight wear. All details sharp.*

	Quan. Minted	Good	V. Good	Fine	V. Fine
1909 V.D.B. (See page 11)	27,995,000	$ .90	$1.10	$1.30	$1.90
1909S V.D.B.	484,000	100.00	115.00	135.00	150.00
1909	72,702,618	.12	.15	.18	.40
1909S	1,825,000	18.00	20.00	22.00	25.00
1910	146,801,218	.06	.08	.15	.50
1910S	6,045,000	3.25	3.75	4.35	5.50
1911	101,177,787	.06	.10	.25	.70

LINCOLN CENTS

	Quan. Minted	Good	V. Good	Fine	V. Fine
1911D	12,672,000	$1.40	$1.75	$2.65	$5.00
1911S	4,026,000	5.75	6.50	7.50	10.00
1912	68,153,060	.06	.14	.40	.85
1912D	10,411,000	1.50	2.00	2.85	5.50
1912S	4,431,000	4.25	5.25	6.50	8.75
1913	76,532,352	.05	.11	.25	.80
1913D	15,804,000	.65	.90	1.75	3.75
1913S	6,101,000	3.00	3.50	4.00	5.50
1914	75,238,432	.07	.13	.45	1.00
1914D*	1,193,000	38.00	42.00	48.00	75.00
1914S	4,137,000	3.75	4.50	5.00	6.75
1915	29,092,120	.30	.50	1.65	3.50
1915D	22,050,000	.30	.45	.85	2.35
1915S	4,833,000	3.10	3.60	4.25	5.50
1916	131,833,677	.03	.06	.10	.30
1916D	35,956,000	.10	.14	.40	1.00
1916S	22,510,000	.30	.40	.65	1.25
1917	196,429,785	.03	.05	.10	.25
1917D	55,120,000	.08	.12	.30	.90
1917S	32,620,000	.10	.15	.30	.90
1918	288,104,634	.04	.08	.12	.25
1918D	47,830,000	.12	.17	.35	.90
1918S	34,680,000	.12	.17	.30	.85
1919	392,021,000	.03	.06	.10	.25
1919D	57,154,000	.10	.15	.25	.65
1919S	139,760,000	.07	.13	.20	.50
1920	310,165,000	.03	.06	.10	.23
1920D	49,280,000	.10	.15	.25	.55
1920S	46,220,000	.10	.15	.25	.50
1921	39,157,000	.10	.15	.30	.50
1921S	15,274,000	.35	.45	.70	2.15
1922D	} 7,160,000	2.60	3.25	4.00	6.00
1922** without D (error)		50.00	65.00	85.00	120.00
1923	74,723,000	.04	.05	.12	.30
1923S	8,700,000	.75	.85	1.75	3.50
1924	75,178,000	.04	.05	.12	.25
1924D	2,520,000	5.25	6.25	7.50	10.00
1924S	11,696,000	.25	.40	.60	1.50
1925	139,949,000	.04	.05	.12	.25
1925D	22,580,000	.08	.12	.25	.50
1925S	26,380,000	.08	.12	.25	.50
1926	157,088,000	.04	.05	.12	.25
1926D	28,020,000	.08	.12	.25	.50
1926S	4,550,000	1.50	1.75	2.25	3.50
1927	144,440,000	.03	.04	.10	.20
1927D	27,170,000	.06	.10	.20	.40
1927S	14,276,000	.20	.30	.50	.90
1928	134,116,000	.03	.04	.10	.20
1928D	31,170,000	.05	.07	.15	.25
1928S	17,266,000	.12	.17	.35	.65
1929	185,262,000	.03	.04	.10	.20
1929D	41,730,000	.03	.04	.10	.20

*Beware of altered date. No VDB on genuine 1914D coin.
**Beware of removed D; see page 31.

LINCOLN CENTS

	Quan. Minted	Good	V. Good	Fine	V. Fine
1929S	50,148,000	$ .03	$ .04	$ .10	$ .20
1930	157,415,000	.03	.04	.08	.12
1930D	40,100,000	.05	.08	.11	.20
1930S	24,286,000	.05	.08	.12	.20
1931	19,396,000	.15	.20	.30	.40
1931D	4,480,000	1.65	1.90	2.10	2.50
1931S	866,000	18.00	20.00	22.00	24.00
1932	9,062,000	.70	.80	1.10	1.70
1932D	10,500,000	.30	.35	.40	.75
1933	14,360,000	.20	.30	.35	.50
1933D	6,200,000	1.00	1.15	1.40	2.00
1934	219,080,000	.02	.02	.03	.04
1934D	28,446,000	.08	.09	.10	.11
1935	245,388,000	.02	.02	.03	.04
1935D	47,000,000	.02	.02	.03	.05
1935S	38,702,000	.02	.02	.04	.06
Proof quantities shown in parentheses					
1936 (5,569)	309,637,569	.02	.02	.03	.04
1936D	40,620,000	.02	.02	.03	.05
1936S	29,130,000	.02	.03	.04	.07
1937 (9,320)	309,179,320	.02	.02	.03	.04
1937D	50,430,000	.02	.02	.03	.05
1937S	34,500,000	.02	.03	.04	.05
1938 (14,734)	156,696,734	.02	.02	.03	.04
1938D	20,010,000	.02	.03	.04	.10
1938S	15,180,000	.10	.12	.15	.18
1939 (13,520)	316,479,520	.02	.02	.03	.04
1939D	15,160,000	.05	.10	.16	.20
1939S	52,070,000	.02	.02	.03	.05
1940 (15,872)	586,825,872	.01	.02	.03	.04
1940D	81,390,000	.01	.02	.03	.05
1940S	112,940,000	.02	.02	.03	.05
1941 (21,100)	887,039,100	.01	.02	.02	.02
1941D	128,700,000	.01	.02	.03	.05
1941S	92,360,000	.02	.02	.03	.05
1942 (32,600)	657,828,600	.01	.02	.02	.02
1942D	206,698,000	.01	.02	.02	.02
1942S	85,590,000	.02	.02	.03	.05

Variety 2 — Zinc-coated steel 1943 only

No bronze cents were officially issued in 1943, although a few may have been struck in error. The steel cents of 1943 will be attracted to a magnet while bronze cents will not.

		V. Good	Fine	V. Fine	Ex. F.
1943	684,628,670	$ .02	$ .04	$ .05	$ .10
1943D	217,660,000	.03	.05	.12	.15
1943S	191,550,000	.03	.05	.12	.15

Variety 1 resumed 1944-1958

1944	1,435,400,000	.01	.02	.02	.02
1944D	430,578,000	.01	.02	.02	.02
1944S	282,760,000	.02	.02	.02	.02
1945	1,040,515,000	.01	.02	.02	.02
1945D	226,268,000	.01	.02	.02	.02
1945S	181,770,000	.02	.02	.02	.02

LINCOLN CENTS

	Quan. Minted	V. Fine	Ex. Fine
1946	991,655,000	$ .02	$ .02
1946D	315,690,000	.02	.02
1946S	198,100,000	.02	.02
1947	190,555,000	.02	.02
1947D	194,750,000	.02	.02
1947S	99,000,000	.02	.04
1948	317,570,000	.02	.02
1948D	172,637,500	.02	.02
1948S	81,735,000	.02	.04
1949	217,775,000	.02	.02
1949D	153,132,500	.02	.02
1949S	64,290,000	.02	.05
1950 (51,386)	272,686,386	.02	.02
1950D	334,950,000	.02	.02
1950S	118,505,000	.02	.03
1951 (57,500)	284,633,500	.02	.02
1951D	625,355,000	.02	.02
1951S	136,010,000	.02	.03
1952 (81,980)	186,856,980	.02	.02
1952D	746,130,000	.02	.02
1952S	137,800,004	.02	.03
1953 (128,800)	256,883,800	.02	.02
1953D	700,515,000	.02	.02
1953S	181,835,000	.02	.03
1954 (233,300)	71,873,350	.02	.05
1954D	251,552,500	.02	.02
1954S	96,190,000	.02	.04
1955 (378,200)	330,958,200	.02	.02
1955 "Doubled die" obverse (error, see picture p. 12)		175.00	200.00
1955D	563,257,500	.02	.02
1955S	44,610,000	.12	.17
1956 (669,384)	421,414,384	.02	.02
1956D	1,098,201,100	.02	.02
1957 (1,247,952)	283,787,952	.02	.02
1957D	1,051,342,000	.02	.02
1958 (875,652)	253,400,652	.02	.02
1958D	800,953,300	.02	.02

LINCOLN TYPE, MEMORIAL REVERSE 1959 to Date

Chief Mint Engraver Frank Gasparro designed the Lincoln Memorial reverse which was introduced in 1959 on the 150th anniversary of Lincoln's birth. Gasparro's initials FG are located to the right of the bottom level of the Memorial.

	Quan. Minted	V. Fine	Ex. Fine
1959 (1,149,291)	610,864,291	.01	.01
1959D	1,279,760,000	.01	.01
1960 Large date (Proofs all kinds 1,691,602)	} 588,096,602	.01	.01
1960 Small date		1.00	1.25
1960D Large date	} 1,580,884,000	.01	.01
1960D Small date (see picture on page 12)		.01	.02

LINCOLN CENTS

	Quan. Minted	Ex. Fine		Quan. Minted	Ex. Fine
1961 (3,028,244)....	756,373,244	$ .01	1972 "Doubled die"		$100.00
1961D	1,753,266,700	.01	1972D	2,665,071,400	.01
1962 (3,218,019)....	609,263,019	.01	1972S (3,260,996) ..	380,200,104	.01
1962D	1,793,148,400	.01	1973	3,728,245,000	.01
1963 (3,075,645)....	757,185,645	.01	1973D	3,549,576,588	.01
1963D	1,774,020,400	.01	1973S (2,760,339) ..	319,937,634	.01
1964 (3,950,762)...	2,652,525,762	.01	1974.............	4,232,140,523	.01
1964D	3,799,071,500	.01	1974D	4,235,098,000	.01
1965	1,497,224,900	.01	1974S (2,612,568) ..	412,039,228	.01
1966	2,188,147,783	.01	1975	5,451,476,142	.01
1967	3,048,667,100	.01	1975D	4,505,275,300	.01
1968	1,707,880,970	.01	1975S Proof only ...	(2,845,450)	8.00
1968D	2,886,296,600	.01	1976	4,674,292,426	.01
1968S.............	261,311,510	.01	1976D	4,221,592,455	.01
1969	1,136,910,000	.01	1976S Proof only ...	(4,149,730)	2.50
1969D	4,002,832,200	.01	1977	4,469,930,000	.01
1969S (2,934,631) ..	547,309,631	.01	1977D	4,194,062,300	.01
1970.............	1,898,315,000	.01	1977S Proof only ...	(3,251,152)	2.50
1970D	2,891,438,900	.01	1978.............	5,558,605,000	.01
1970S (2,632,810) ..	693,192,814	.01	1978D	4,280,233,400	.01
1971.............	1,919,490,000	.01	1978S Proof only ...	(3,127,781)	2.50
1971D	2,911,045,600	.01	1979		.01
1971S (3,220,733) ..	528,345,192	.01	1979D		.01
1972.............	2,933,255,000	.01	1979S Proof only		2.50

"HARD TIMES" AND CIVIL WAR TOKENS

In addition to the coins issued by the United States government, numismatists include in their collection the "Hard Times" and Civil War tokens which circulated as money during two periods in this country's history when nearly all the minor coin was hoarded.

The Hard Times tokens were issued in the period 1834-1844 and are the size of the U.S. large size cent. They were generally struck in copper in two general groups: political tokens whose theme centered around President Jackson's fight against the United States Bank, and those issued by merchants (tradesmen's cards). Common varieties are worth 50¢ to $1.00 each.

During the Civil War small coin was again hoarded; millions of privately coined tokens of political or advertising nature were placed in circulation. Some 10,000 different varieties have been discovered, most of which are more or less common and worth from 50¢ to $1.00 each. A large majority of the Civil War tokens are about the same size as the present day one-cent piece.

All Cents of 1922 Struck at Denver

An explanation of the 1922 cent without mint mark D was published some years ago. Apparently the die from which these coins were struck became worn and the D beneath the date did not appear on several hundred coins released for actual circulation.

The number of coins released without the mint mark was very small and therefore they are worth many times the value of those coins with the mint mark showing.

TWO-CENT BRONZE
Issued from 1864 through 1873

Those of 1864 are of two varieties: small letters in the motto, "In God We Trust," and the second variety has the same letters in a slightly larger size. Those of the large motto variety are the commonest of the two-cent pieces, while the small motto is the rarest. It is a little difficult to distinguish the two sizes of mottos without some study. The D in GOD is wide in proportion to its height on the small motto variety (see page 11). The two-cent piece was the first United States coin to bear the motto, "In God We Trust."

GOOD—*At least IN GOD visible.*
V. GOOD—*WE weakly visible.*
FINE—*Complete Motto visible. WE weak.*
EX. FINE—*WE is bold.*

	Quan. Minted	Good	V. Good	Fine	Ex. Fine
1864 Small motto	⎫ 19,847,500	$25.00	$35.00	$42.00	$100.00
Large motto	⎭	3.00	3.75	5.00	20.00
1865	13,640,000	3.00	3.75	5.00	20.00
1866	3,177,000	3.00	4.00	6.00	22.00
1867	2,938,750	3.00	4.00	6.00	22.00
1868	2,803,750	3.00	4.00	6.00	22.00
1869	1,546,500	3.25	4.50	7.00	22.00
1870	861,250	4.00	5.00	8.00	23.00
1871	721,250	5.00	7.00	11.00	25.00
1872	65,000	25.00	33.00	50.00	80.00
					Proof
1873 Proofs only					550.00

NICKEL THREE-CENT PIECES
Issued from 1865 through 1889

This coinage was authorized for the purpose of retiring the 3-cent fractional currency notes. All dates are of the same type. The two rarest dates are 1877 and 1878, both of which were struck in proof only. A variety of 1887 has the date engraved over "86."

GOOD—*Date and legends complete though worn. III smooth.*
V. GOOD—*III is half worn. Rims complete.*
FINE—*Hair curls well defined.*
EX. FINE—*Slight, even wear.*

	Quan. Minted	Good	V. Good	Fine	Ex. Fine
1865	11,382,000	$3.00	$3.50	$4.25	$9.50
1866	4,801,000	3.00	3.50	4.25	10.00
1867	3,915,000	3.00	3.50	4.25	10.00
1868	3,252,000	3.00	3.50	4.25	10.00
1869	1,604,000	3.00	3.50	4.25	10.00

NICKEL THREE-CENT PIECES

	Quan. Minted	Good	V. Good	Fine	Ex. Fine	Proof
1870 1,335,000		$3.00	$3.50	$4.50	$12.00	
1871 604,000		3.25	4.00	5.00	13.00	
1872 862,000		3.25	4.00	5.00	13.00	
1873 1,173,000		3.00	3.50	4.50	12.00	
1874 790,000		3.25	4.00	5.00	13.00	
1875 228,000		4.25	5.25	7.00	15.00	
1876 162,000		4.25	5.25	7.00	15.00	
1877 Proofs only						$550.00
1878 Proofs only 2,350						250.00
1879 41,200		13.00	17.00	22.00	30.00	150.00
1880 24,955		14.00	19.00	25.00	35.00	150.00
1881 1,080,575		3.00	3.50	4.25	10.00	130.00
1882 25,300		14.00	19.00	25.00	35.00	150.00
1883 10,609		20.00	25.00	30.00	55.00	150.00
1884 5,642		25.00	30.00	40.00	65.00	175.00
1885 4,790		27.00	35.00	45.00	70.00	175.00
1886 Proofs only 4,290						200.00
1887 7 over 6 (Proofs only)						250.00
1887 Normal date 7,961		30.00	35.00	45.00	70.00	200.00
1888 41,083		13.00	17.00	23.00	33.00	135.00
1889 21,561		13.00	17.00	23.00	33.00	135.00

FIVE-CENT NICKELS

Issued from 1866 to date

Five-cent nickel coins were authorized for the purpose of retiring fractional currency notes of denominations less than 10 cents.

The first type is known as the "shield type" and has two varieties; both 1866 and 1867 have rays through the stars (1867 also was coined without the rays). Proofs only were coined for the years 1877 and 1878, the former being the rarest date of the shield type and also of the entire 5-cent nickel series, except 1913.

In 1883 the type was changed to the more or less familiar "Liberty head." This type first appeared without the word CENTS on the coin; merely a large letter "V" to denote denomination. As this coin is about the size of a five-dollar gold piece these "cent-less" nickels were immediately gold-plated and passed on unsuspecting people for five dollars. Later in the year the word CENTS was added. The cent-less variety was hoarded in great numbers and frequently turns up today. 1885 and 1912S mint are the rarest dates of this type.

The 1913 Liberty Head Nickel did not become known to the numismatic world until 1920, when five specimens were exhibited at a meeting of coin collectors in Chicago. Very clever fake 1913's have been made by altering 1903 and 1910 nickels.

Indian Head type nickels were first coined in 1913 with the buffalo or "bison" standing on "raised" ground. This is known as Variety 1; the ground or plane was recessed to form Variety 2.

In 1938 the Treasury of the United States announced a public competition for a new design, it being specified that the head of Jefferson and a reproduction of his home, Monticello, be the important features. Some 390 entries were received and Felix Schlag of Chicago won the $1,000 prize.

FIVE-CENT NICKELS
SHIELD TYPE 1866-1883

Rays between stars 1866-1867   Without Rays 1867-1883

GOOD—*All letters in Motto readable.*
V. GOOD—*Motto stands out clearly. Rims worn slightly but even. Part of shield lines visible.*
FINE—*Half of each olive leaf is smooth.*
EX. FINE—*Leaf tips show slight wear. Cross over shield slightly worn.*

	Quan. Minted	Good	V. Good	Fine	Ex. Fine
1866 Rays through stars	14,742,500	$6.00	$8.00	$13.00	$50.00
1867 Rays......................	2,019,000	7.00	9.50	17.50	55.00
Without Rays..............	28,890,500	4.25	5.00	6.50	20.00
1868	28,817,000	4.25	5.00	6.50	20.00
1869	16,395,000	4.25	5.00	6.50	20.00
1870	4,806,000	5.00	6.00	9.00	23.00
1871	561,000	17.00	21.00	35.00	67.50
1872	6,036,000	5.00	6.00	8.00	20.00
1873	4,550,000	5.00	6.00	8.00	20.00
1874	3,538,000	5.50	6.50	9.00	22.00
1875	2,097,000	7.50	9.00	14.00	34.00
1876	2,530,000	7.00	8.00	13.00	30.00
1877 Proofs only............	estimated 500			Proof	725.00
1878 Proofs only.............	2,350			Proof	235.00
1879	29,100	30.00	40.00	50.00	70.00
1880	19,955	40.00	47.50	55.00	80.00
1881	72,375	30.00	40.00	50.00	65.00
1882	11,476,600	4.25	5.00	6.50	18.00
1883 Shield type...............	1,456,919	4.25	5.00	6.50	18.00

LIBERTY HEAD TYPE 1883-1913

Without CENTS 1883   With CENTS 1881-1912

GOOD—*No detail in head. LIBERTY obliterated.*
V. GOOD—*At least 3 letters in LIBERTY readable.*
FINE—*All letters in LIBERTY show.*
EX. FINE—*LIBERTY sharp. Corn grains at bottom of wreath show, on reverse.*

FIVE-CENT NICKELS

	Quan. Minted	Good	V. Good	Fine	Ex. Fine
1883 Liberty, without CENTS	5,479,519	$1.00	$1.50	$2.25	$5.00
1883 Liberty, with CENTS.......	16,032,983	3.00	4.00	6.00	15.00
1884	11,273,942	3.00	4.00	6.00	16.00
1885	1,476,490	65.00	75.00	120.00	165.00
1886	3,330,290	22.00	27.00	43.00	75.00
1887	15,263,652	1.65	2.00	3.75	12.00
1888	10,720,483	2.25	3.50	6.00	15.00
1889	15,881,361	1.50	2.25	4.00	12.00
1890	16,259,272	1.50	2.50	4.50	12.00
1891	16,834,350	1.50	2.00	3.75	12.00
1892	11,699,642	1.50	2.00	4.00	12.00
1893	13,370,195	1.35	2.00	3.75	11.00
1894	5,413,132	2.25	3.25	6.00	15.00
1895	9,979,884	1.25	2.00	3.00	11.00
1896	8,842,920	1.25	2.00	3.50	12.00
1897	20,428,735	.40	.55	1.25	8.00
1898	12,532,087	.40	.55	1.25	8.00
1899	26,029,031	.40	.55	1.25	8.00
1900	27,255,995	.25	.35	.75	7.00
1901	26,480,213	.25	.35	.75	7.00
1902	31,480,579	.25	.35	.75	7.00
1903	28,006,725	.25	.35	.75	7.00
1904	21,404,984	.25	.35	.75	7.00
1905	29,827,276	.25	.35	.75	7.00
1906	38,613,725	.25	.35	.75	7.00
1907	39,214,800	.25	.35	.75	7.00
1908	22,686,177	.25	.35	.75	7.00
1909	11,590,526	.30	.50	.90	7.00
1910	30,169,353	.25	.35	.75	7.00
1911	39,559,372	.25	.35	.75	7.00
1912	26,236,714	.25	.35	.75	7.00
1912D..........................	8,474,000	.50	.75	2.00	30.00
1912S..........................	238,000	20.00	23.00	30.00	100.00

1913 Liberty Head (not a regular issue, beware altered date). ——

INDIAN HEAD or BUFFALO TYPE 1913-1938

James E. Fraser, who designed the Buffalo Nickel, used three different Indians to obtain the portrait on the obverse side. The models were Iron Tail, a Sioux warrior; Two Moons, a Cheyenne chief; and John Big Tree, an Onondaga chief. The bison was modeled after "Black Diamond" in the New York Zoological Garden. The famous animal was slaughtered in 1915 and his massive head was preserved and mounted.

Variety 1
Bison on mound

Variety 2
Bison on plane

GOOD—*Legends and date readable. Horn worn off.*
V. GOOD—*Half horn shows.*
FINE—*Three-quarters of horn shows. Obv. rim intact.*
EX. FINE—*Full horn. Slight wear on Indian's hair ribbon.*

[35]

FIVE-CENT NICKELS

16 N/D

	Quan. Minted	Good	V. Good	Fine	Ex. Fine
1913 Indian head — Variety 1 —					
Bison on mound	30,993,520	$1.20	$1.40	$1.75	$5.00
1913D Variety 1	5,337,000	2.70	3.50	4.00	8.00
1913S Variety 1	2,105,000	3.50	4.50	5.75	14.00
1913 Indian Head — Variety 2 —					
Bison on plane.............	29,858,700	1.75	2.00	2.75	5.00
1913D Variety 2.................	4,156,000	14.00	17.00	22.00	35.00
1913S Variety 2	1,209,000	23.00	30.00	35.00	60.00
1914	20,665,738	1.50	2.00	3.00	7.00
1914D........................	3,912,000	12.00	14.00	20.00	40.00
1914S........................	3,470,000	2.50	3.50	5.75	17.00
1915.........................	20,987,270	.60	.80	1.65	5.50
1915D........................	7,569,500	2.85	3.75	6.00	19.00
1915S........................	1,505,000	4.00	6.00	12.00	35.00
1916	63,498,066	.30	.45	.85	4.00
1916D........................	13,333,000	2.00	2.50	4.00	14.00
1916S........................	11,860,000	1.50	2.00	3.50	14.00
1917.........................	51,424,029	.25	.50	1.00	4.50
1917D........................	9,910,800	1.75	3.00	5.75	30.00
1917S........................	4,193,000	1.75	3.00	5.75	30.00
1918	32,086,314	.30	.50	1.15	7.00
1918D 8 over 7 .... } 8,362,000	140.00	200.00	350.00	1200.00
Normal date.............. }	2.00	3.00	6.00	35.00
1918S........................	4,882,000	1.50	2.75	5.00	32.00
1919	60,868,000	.30	.40	.80	4.00
1919D........................	8,006,000	1.75	3.50	6.75	50.00
1919S........................	7,521,000	1.50	3.00	5.50	45.00
1920	63,093,000	.25	.35	.75	4.50
1920D........................	9,418,000	1.50	2.50	5.50	37.50
1920S........................	9,689,000	.90	1.75	4.00	35.00
1921.........................	10,663,000	.35	.55	1.25	6.50
1921S........................	1,557,000	5.00	8.25	17.00	70.00
1923	35,715,000	.20	.30	.55	3.50
1923S........................	6,142,000	.65	1.20	3.50	30.00
1924	21,620,000	.15	.25	.50	4.00
1924D........................	5,258,000	.80	1.25	3.75	34.00
1924S........................	1,437,000	2.00	3.25	9.00	90.00
1925	35,565,100	.15	.25	.50	4.00
1925D........................	4,450,000	1.50	3.00	6.00	37.50
1925S........................	6,256,000	1.10	2.25	5.00	30.00
1926	44,693,000	.10	.13	.25	3.00
1926D........................	5,638,000	1.00	1.75	4.25	32.00
1926S........................	970,000	2.75	4.25	7.50	85.00
1927	37,981,000	.07	.12	.20	2.50
1927D........................	5,730,000	.30	.65	1.50	12.00
1927S........................	3,430,000	.45	.90	2.50	27.50
1928	23,411,000	.07	.12	.20	2.25
1928D........................	6,436,000	.15	.30	.65	3.75
1928S........................	6,936,000	.20	.35	.70	4.75
1929	36,446,000	.07	.12	.20	1.75
1929D........................	8,370,000	.15	.25	.45	2.50
1929S........................	7,754,000	.15	.25	.45	2.00
1930	22,849,000	.07	.12	.20	1.50
1930S........................	5,435,000	.20	.35	.80	2.75

FIVE-CENT NICKELS

	Quan. Minted	Good	V. Good	Fine	Ex. Fine
1931S	1,200,000	$1.50	$2.00	$2.75	$8.00
1934	20,213,003	.07	.10	.20	1.50
1934D	7,480,000	.10	.15	.30	3.00
1935	58,264,000	.07	.10	.15	.85
1935D	12,092,000	.07	.10	.15	1.50
1935S	10,300,000	.07	.10	.15	1.00
1936 (Proofs 4,420)	119,001,420	.07	.10	.15	.65
1936D	24,814,000	.07	.10	.15	.85
1936S	14,930,000	.07	.10	.15	.75
1937(Proofs 5,769)	79,485,769	.07	.10	.15	.65
1937D Normal	} 17,826,000	.07	.10	.15	.75
1937D* Three-legged Buffalo		55.00	65.00	75.00	100.00
1937S	5,635,000	.10	.15	.20	.90
1938D Buffalo — All kinds	7,020,000	.07	.10	.15	.80
1938D over S (See illustration page 12).				2.50	5.00

*Beware of alterations (removed leg).

JEFFERSON TYPE 1938 to Date

The design of this nickel is by Felix Schlag, who won a $1,000 prize for his entry. It is established public acceptance of portrait and pictorial devices on our coinage. Schlag's initials FS were placed on the coin beginning in 1966, below the bust.

VERY GOOD—*Second porch pillar from right nearly gone, other three still visible but weak.*

EX. FINE—*Cheekbone, hairlines, eyebrow slightly worn but well defined. Base of triangle above pillars visible but weak.*

	Quan. Minted	Very Good	Ex. Fine		Quan. Minted	Very Good	Ex. Fine
1938 (Proofs 19,365)				1940D	43,540,000	$ .05	$ .07
Jefferson	19,515,365	$ .07	$ .20	1940S	39,690,000	.05	.10
1938D	5,376,000	.50	1.00	1941 (Proofs 18,720)			
1938S	4,105,000	1.00	2.10		203,283,720	.05	.07
1939 (Proofs 12,535)				1941D	53,432,000	.05	.10
	120,627,535	.05	.07	1941S	43,445,000	.05	.10
1939D	3,514,000	2.40	5.00	1942 (Proofs 29,600)			
1939S	6,630,000	.35	1.20		49,818,600	.05	.07
1940 (Proofs 14,158)				1942D	13,938,000	.10	.35
	176,499,158	.05	.07				

FIVE-CENT NICKELS
WARTIME SILVER FIVE-CENT PIECES 1942-1945
(Mint mark above dome on reverse side)
All nickels before 1956 have a premium in bright uncirculated condition.

Quan. Minted	Very Good	Ex. Fine		Quan. Minted	Very Good	Ex. Fine
1942P (Proofs 27,600)			1944P...... 119,150,000	$ .35	$ .45
.... 57,900,600	$ .35	$ .45	1944D 32,309,000	.35	.45
1942S........ 32,900,000	.35	.50	1944S........ 21,640,000	.35	.45
1943P...... 271,165,000	.35	.45	1945P...... 119,408,100	.35	.45
1943D 15,294,000	.40	1.00	1945D 37,158,000	.35	.45
1943S...... 104,060,000	.35	.45	1945S........ 58,939,000	.35	.45

PREWAR COPPER-NICKEL COMPOSITION RESUMED

Quan. Minted	Ex. F.		Quan. Minted	Ex. F.
1946................ 161,116,000	$ .05		1962D 280,195,720	$ .05
1946D 45,292,200	.05		1963 (3,075,645)...... 178,851,645	.05
1946S............... 13,560,000	.15		1963D 276,829,460	.05
1947................ 95,000,000	.05		1964 (3,950,762).... 1,028,622,762	.05
1947D 37,822,000	.05		1964D 1,787,297,160	.05
1947S............... 24,720,000	.10		1965 136,131,380	.05
1948................ 89,348,000	.05		1966................ 156,208,283	.05
1948D............... 44,734,000	.08		1967 107,325,800	.05
1948S............... 11,300,000	.15		1968D 91,227,880	.05
1949................ 60,652,000	.05		1968S............. 103,437,510	.05
1949D 36,498,000	.05		1969D 202,807,500	.05
1949S............... 9,716,000	.15		1969S (2,934,631) 123,099,631	.05
1950 (51,386) 9,847,386	.20		1970D 515,485,380	.05
1950D 2,630,030	5.50		1970S (2,632,810) 241,464,814	.05
1951 (57,500) 28,609,500	.05		1971 106,884,000	.05
1951D 20,460,000	.05		1971D 316,144,800	.05
1951S................ 7,776,000	.45		1971S Proof only .... (3,220,733)	.60
1952 (81,980) 64,069,980	.05		1972................ 202,036,000	.05
1952D 30,638,000	.08		1972D 351,094,600	.05
1952S............... 20,572,000	.08		1972S Proof only .... (3,260,996)	.60
1953 (128,800) 46,772,800	.05		1973 384,396,000	.05
1953D 59,878,600	.05		1973D 261,405,400	.05
1953S............... 19,210,900	.08		1973S Proof only .... (2,760,339)	.75
1954 (233,300) 47,917,350	.05		1974 601,752,000	.05
1954D 117,183,060	.05		1974D 277,373,000	.05
1954S............... 29,384,000	.05		1974S Proof only .... (2,612,568)	1.60
1955 (378,200) 8,266,200	.30		1975 181,772,000	.05
1955D 74,464,100	.05		1975D 401,875,300	.05
1956 (669,384) 35,885,384	.05		1975S Proof only .... (2,845,450)	1.00
1956D 67,222,940	.05		1976................ 367,124,000	.05
1957 (1,247,952)....... 39,655,952	.05		1976D 563,964,147	.05
1957D 136,828,900	.05		1976S Proof only .... (4,149,730)	.60
1958 (875,652) 17,963,652	.10		1977 585,376,000	.05
1958D 168,249,120	.05		1977D 297,313,422	.05
1959 (1,149,291)....... 28,397,291	.05		1977S Proof only .... (3,251,152)	.90
1959D 160,738,240	.05		1978................ 391,308,000	.05
1960 (1,691,602)....... 57,107,602	.05		1978D 313,092,780	.05
1960D 192,582,180	.05		1978S Proof only .... (3,127,781)	.90
1961 (3,028,244)....... 76,668,244	.05		1979	.05
1961D 229,342,760	.05		1979D	.05
1962 (3,218,019)...... 100,602,019	.05		1979S Proof only	.90

SILVER THREE-CENT PIECES

Issued from 1851 through 1873

This smallest of United States silver coins was authorized to facilitate postal transactions; however, because of its small size it became unpopular.

The same general design was used throughout the entire coinage except for some minor changes in design and alloy. In 1854 the size of the star on the obverse was enlarged as was the size of the date, and arrows and branches were added. In 1859 the outlines on the star were reduced from three to two and the size of the date was reduced.

GOOD—*Star worn smooth. Legend and date readable.*
V. GOOD—*Outline of shield defined. Legend and date clear.*
FINE—*Only star points worn smooth.*
V. FINE—*Only partial wear on star ridges.*

	Quan. Minted	Good	V. Good	Fine	V. Fine
Variety 1: No outline around star					
1851	5,447,400	$4.50	$6.50	$9.00	$15.00
1851O	720,000	6.25	9.00	15.00	28.00
1852	18,663,500	4.25	6.00	8.00	14.00
1853	11,400,000	4.25	6.00	8.00	14.00
Variety 2: Three outlines to star, large date					
1854	671,000	6.25	8.00	12.00	21.00
1855	139,000	8.50	11.50	18.00	33.00
1856	1,458,000	6.00	7.50	12.00	20.00
1857	1,042,000	6.00	7.50	12.00	20.00
1858	1,604,000	6.00	7.50	12.00	20.00
Variety 3: Two outlines to star, small date					
1859	365,000	6.25	7.50	12.00	20.00
1860	287,000	6.25	7.50	12.00	20.00
1861	498,000	6.00	7.50	12.00	20.00
1862	343,550	6.00	7.50	12.00	20.00

		Unc.	Proof
1863	21,460	$300.00	$300.00
1864	12,470	275.00	300.00
1865	8,500	250.00	275.00
1866	22,725	250.00	275.00
1867	4,625	250.00	275.00
1868	4,100	250.00	275.00
1869	5,100	250.00	275.00
1870	4,000	250.00	275.00
1871	4,360	250.00	275.00
1872	1,950	250.00	275.00
1873 Proofs only	600		375.00

HALF DIMES—Issued from 1794 to 1873

Coinage for general circulation started with 1794 although some believe the 1792 half disme to be a regular issue (see page 3). All the early dates, those before 1829, are more or less rare, with the 1802 being one of the great United States silver rarities.

Die varieties are numerous in this series; one curious variety is that of the year 1800 where the word "Liberty" appears to be spelled "LIBEKTY."

Abbreviations used in describing half dimes (those not previously explained in preceding pages) are:

Ars. — arrows. (Arrows at the date on 1853, 1854 and 1855.)

Drap. — drapery. (Drapery on the left elbow of Liberty.)

	Quan. Minted	Fair	Good	V. Good	Fine	V. Fine
1792 Half Disme		$325.00	$600.00	$850.00	$1,350	$2,200

FLOWING HAIR TYPE 1794-1795

FAIR—*Details clear enough to identify.*
GOOD—*Eagle, wreath, bust outlined but lack details.*
V. GOOD—*Some details remain on face. All lettering readable.*
FINE—*Hair ends show. Hair at top smooth.*
V. FINE—*Hairlines at top show. Hair about ear defined.*

1794 ⎱ 86,416	90.00	200.00	270.00	425.00	685.00
1795 ⎰	85.00	190.00	235.00	350.00	500.00

DRAPED BUST TYPE, SMALL EAGLE REVERSE 1796-1797

FAIR—*Details clear enough to identify.*
GOOD—*Date, stars, LIBERTY readable. Bust outlined but no details.*
V. GOOD—*Some details show.*
FINE—*Hair and drapery lines worn, but visible.*
V. FINE—*Only left of drapery indistinct.*

1796 10,230	100.00	235.00	300.00	400.00	600.00
1797 15 stars .... ⎱	90.00	200.00	275.00	375.00	550.00
16 stars .... ⎬ 44,527	90.00	200.00	275.00	375.00	550.00
13 stars .... ⎰	90.00	200.00	275.00	375.00	550.00

DRAPED BUST TYPE, HERALDIC EAGLE REVERSE 1800-1805

1800 Normal Obv. .... ⎱ 24,000	75.00	165.00	200.00	300.00	475.00
LIBEKTY var ...... ⎰	75.00	165.00	200.00	300.00	475.00

[40]

HALF DIMES

	Quan. Minted	Fair	Good	V. Good	Fine	V. Fine
1801	33,910	$75.00	$165.00	$200.00	$315.00	$475.00
1802 (Rare)	13,010	675.00	1,500	2,400	3,750	6,500
1803	37,850	75.00	165.00	200.00	315.00	450.00
1805	15,600	95.00	200.00	270.00	375.00	650.00

CAPPED BUST TYPE 1829-1837

GOOD—*Bust outlined, no detail. Date and legend readable.*
V. GOOD—*Complete legend and date plain. At least 3 letters of LIBERTY show clearly.*
FINE—*All letters in LIBERTY show.*
V. FINE—*Full rim, both sides. Clasp on shoulder and ear well defined.*

	Quan. Minted	Good	V. Good	Fine	V. Fine
1829	1,230,000	10.00	12.50	15.00	21.00
1830	1,240,000	9.75	12.25	14.50	20.00
1831	1,242,700	9.75	12.25	14.50	20.00
1832	965,000	9.75	12.25	14.50	20.00
1833	1,370,000	9.75	12.25	14.50	20.00
1834	1,480,000	9.75	12.25	14.50	20.00
1835	2,760,000	9.75	12.25	14.50	20.00
1836	1,900,000	9.75	12.25	14.50	20.00
1837	both types 2,276,000	9.75	12.25	14.50	20.00

LIBERTY SEATED TYPE 1837-1873
Variety 1 — No stars on obverse 1837-1838

GOOD—*LIBERTY on shield smooth. Date and letters readable.*
V. GOOD—*At least 3 letters in LIBERTY are visible.*
FINE—*Entire LIBERTY visible, weak spots.*
V. FINE—*Entire LIBERTY strong and even.*

		Good	V. Good	Fine	V. Fine
1837 No stars	inc. above	20.00	27.50	42.00	65.00
1838O No stars	70,000	25.00	35.00	50.00	90.00

Variety 2 — Stars on obverse 1838-1859

		Good	V. Good	Fine	V. Fine
1838 With stars	2,255,000	3.35	4.00	6.00	11.00
1839	1,069,150	3.35	4.00	6.00	11.00
1839O	1,034,039	4.50	6.00	7.50	16.00
1840	1,344,085	3.50	4.25	6.50	11.00
1840O	935,000	4.25	6.00	8.00	17.00
1841	1,150,000	3.35	4.25	6.50	11.00
1841O	815,000	4.00	5.00	7.00	13.00
1842	815,000	3.50	4.50	6.50	11.00
1842O	350,000	5.00	7.00	12.00	25.00
1843	1,165,000	3.35	4.25	6.50	11.00
1844	430,000	4.00	5.00	8.00	13.00
1844O	220,000	6.50	9.00	15.00	40.00

HALF DIMES

	Quan. Minted	Good	V. Good	Fine	V. Fine
1845	1,564,000	$3.35	$4.00	$6.00	$10.00
1846	27,000	34.00	42.50	60.00	100.00
1847	1,274,000	3.35	4.00	6.00	10.00
1848	668,000	3.35	4.00	6.00	10.00
1848O	600,000	4.50	6.00	10.00	22.00
1849	1,309,000	3.35	4.00	6.00	10.00
1849O	140,000	15.00	23.00	33.00	67.50
1850	955,000	3.35	4.00	6.00	10.00
1850O	690,000	4.00	5.00	9.00	18.00
1851	781,000	3.35	4.00	6.00	10.00
1851O	860,000	4.00	5.00	9.00	18.00
1852	1,000,500	3.35	4.00	6.00	10.00
1852O	260,000	5.00	9.00	16.00	30.00
1853 No arrows	135,000	7.50	10.00	18.00	30.00
1853O No arrows	160,000	45.00	57.50	90.00	150.00

Variety 3 — Arrows at date 1853-1855

Arrows at either side of date were added to indicate reduction of weight. Genuine specimens without arrows should weigh more than specimens with arrows.

1853 With arrows	13,210,020	3.25	4.25	6.25	9.50
1853O With arrows	2,200,000	3.25	4.25	6.25	9.50
1854 Arrows	5,740,000	3.25	4.25	6.25	9.50
1854O Arrows	1,560,000	3.25	4.25	6.25	9.50
1855 Arrows	1,750,000	3.25	4.25	6.25	9.50
1855O Arrows	600,000	4.00	5.00	7.00	15.00

Variety 2 resumed 1856-1859

1856 No arrows	4,880,000	3.25	4.25	5.50	8.50
1856O	1,100,000	3.25	4.25	5.50	8.50
1857	7,280,000	3.25	4.25	5.50	8.50
1857O	1,380,000	3.25	4.25	5.50	8.50
1858	3,500,000	3.25	4.25	5.50	8.50
1858O	1,660,000	3.25	4.25	5.50	8.50
1859	340,000	5.00	8.00	12.00	18.00
1859O	560,000	5.00	8.00	11.00	16.00

In the years 1859 and 1860 a half-dime type was struck which does not bear our nation's identity. These coins are known as transitional patterns, and were struck at the time the inscription UNITED STATES OF AMERICA was being transferred from the reverse to the obverse side of the coin. These coins are not a regular mint issue.

1859 (Obv. of 1859. Rev. of 1860)... Proof $3,750
1860 Stars
   (Obv. of 1859. Rev. of 1860)........ 100 .... Unc. 1,400

Variety 4 — Legend on obverse 1860-1873

1860 Legend	799,000	3.25	4.00	5.50	8.50
1860O Legend	1,060,000	3.25	4.00	5.50	8.50

HALF DIMES

	Quan. Minted	Good	V. Good	Fine	V. Fine
1861	3,361,000	$3.25	$4.00	$5.50	$8.00
1862	1,492,550	3.25	4.00	5.50	8.00
1863	18,460	25.00	32.00	40.00	55.00
1863S	100,000	8.00	10.00	13.00	22.50
1864	48,470	75.00	100.00	115.00	160.00
1864S	90,000	9.00	12.00	16.00	30.00
1865	13,500	25.00	32.00	45.00	60.00
1865S	120,000	5.50	7.00	10.00	19.00
1866	10,725	25.00	32.00	45.00	60.00
1866S	120,000	5.50	7.00	10.00	19.00
1867	8,625	30.00	45.00	55.00	75.00
1867S	120,000	5.50	7.00	10.00	19.00
1868	89,200	6.50	9.00	12.00	23.00
1868S	280,000	3.25	4.00	5.50	10.00
1869	208,600	3.25	4.00	5.50	10.00
1869S	230,000	3.25	4.00	5.50	10.00
1870	536,600	3.25	4.00	5.50	9.00
1870S	(unique)				
1871	1,873,960	3.25	4.00	5.50	8.00
1871S	161,000	6.50	9.00	14.00	25.00
1872	2,947,950	3.25	4.00	5.50	8.00
1872S Mint mark within wreath	} 837,000	3.25	4.00	5.50	8.50
Mint mark below wreath		3.25	4.00	5.50	8.50
1873	712,600	3.25	4.00	5.50	8.50
1873S	324,000	3.25	4.00	5.50	8.50

DIMES

Issued from 1796 to date

The designs of the dimes follow very closely those of the half dime up through the Liberty seated type. Also, in similar fashion to half dime, there is nothing in the design of the early dates to indicate the value of the piece. The early dates are scarce, especially in choice condition.

The Liberty head type issued from 1892 to 1916 was designed by Charles Barber, and each coin has his initial B on the truncation of the neck.

DRAPED BUST TYPE, SMALL EAGLE REVERSE 1796-1797

FAIR—*Details clear enough to identify.*
GOOD—*Date readable. Bust outlined, but no detail.*
V. GOOD—*All but deepest drapery folds worn smooth. Hairlines nearly gone and curls lack detail.*
FINE—*All drapery lines visible. Hair partly worn.*
V. FINE—*Only left side of drapery is indistinct.*

	Quan. Minted	Fair	Good	V. Good	Fine	V. Fine
1796	22,135	$175.00	$325.00	$450.00	$650.00	$1,100
1797 16 stars	} 25,261	135.00	300.00	400.00	600.00	950.00
13 stars		135.00	300.00	400.00	600.00	950.00

DIMES
DRAPED BUST TYPE, HERALDIC EAGLE REVERSE 1798-1807

	Quan. Minted	Fair	Good	V. Good	Fine	V. Fine
1798 All kinds............ 27,550						
8 over 7, 16 stars on Rev.		$55.00	$110.00	$150.00	$235.00	$360.00
8 over 7, 13 stars on Rev.				375.00	600.00	1,100
Normal date..............		55.00	110.00	150.00	235.00	360.00
1800 21,760		50.00	100.00	140.00	225.00	325.00
1801 34,640		50.00	100.00	140.00	225.00	350.00
1802 10,975		60.00	125.00	175.00	250.00	400.00
1803 33,040		50.00	100.00	140.00	225.00	335.00
1804 8,265		130.00	225.00	350.00	550.00	850.00
1805 120,780		45.00	100.00	135.00	190.00	310.00
1807 165,000		45.00	100.00	135.00	190.00	310.00

CAPPED BUST TYPE 1809-1837
Variety 1 — Large size 1809-1828

GOOD—*Date, letters and stars discernible. Bust outlined, no details.*
V. GOOD—*Legends and date plain. Minimum of 3 letters in LIBERTY show.*
FINE—*Full LIBERTY. Ear and shoulder clasp visible. Part of rim shows on both sides.*
V. FINE—*LIBERTY distinct. Full rim. Ear and clasp plain and distinct.*

	Quan. Minted	Good	V. Good	Fine	V. Fine
1809 51,065		32.50	50.00	75.00	140.00
1811 11 over 09..................... 65,180		22.50	27.50	45.00	85.00
1814 421,500		11.00	15.00	22.00	40.00
1820 942,587		10.00	14.00	20.00	35.00
1821 1,186,512		10.00	14.00	20.00	35.00
1822 100,000		30.00	42.50	80.00	150.00
1823 440,000		10.00	14.00	22.00	37.50
1824 4 over 2..................... } 510,000		12.00	17.00	25.00	45.00
1825 .... }		11.00	14.00	22.00	35.00
1827 1,215,000		10.00	13.00	19.00	33.00
1828 Large date .... } 125,000		15.00	22.00	36.00	67.00
Small date .... }		10.00	15.00	22.00	35.00

DIMES
Variety 2 — Reduced size 1829-1837

	Quan. Minted	Good	V. Good	Fine	V. Fine
1829 Small and medium 10c ⎫	770,000	$9.00	$12.00	$17.00	$30.00
Large 10c ⎭		10.00	13.00	21.00	33.00
1830	510,000	8.25	11.00	15.00	24.00
1831	771,350	8.25	11.00	15.00	24.00
1832	522,500	8.25	11.00	15.00	24.00
1833	485,000	8.25	11.00	15.00	24.00
1834	635,000	8.25	11.00	15.00	24.00
1835	1,410,000	8.25	11.00	15.00	24.00
1836	1,190,000	8.25	11.00	15.00	24.00
1837 both types	1,042,000	8.25	11.00	15.00	24.00

LIBERTY SEATED TYPE 1837-1891

GOOD—*LIBERTY on shield smooth. Date and letters readable.*
V. GOOD—*At least 3 letters in LIBERTY are visible.*
FINE—*Entire LIBERTY visible, weak spots.*
V. FINE—*Entire LIBERTY strong and even.*

1837 Liberty seated, no stars		19.00	25.00	42.50	90.00
1838O Liberty seated, no stars	406,034	22.50	32.50	60.00	125.00

Stars on Obverse 1838-1860

1838	1,992,500	3.50	4.50	6.00	10.00
1839	1,053,115	3.50	4.00	5.00	8.50
1839O	1,323,000	3.50	4.50	6.00	13.00
1840	1,358,580	3.00	5.00	8.00	15.00
1840O No drapery	1,175,000	3.50	4.50	6.50	13.00
1841 No drapery ⎫	1,622,500				
1841 Drapery ⎭		2.25	3.25	4.25	8.00
1841O	2,007,500	2.75	4.00	7.00	11.00
1842	1,887,500	2.25	3.25	4.25	8.00
1842O	2,020,000	2.50	3.50	4.50	9.00
1843	1,370,000	2.25	3.25	4.25	8.00
1843O	150,000	14.00	19.00	38.00	150.00
1844	72,500	16.00	25.00	42.00	95.00
1845	1,755,000	2.25	3.25	4.25	8.00
1845O	230,000	5.00	8.50	15.00	50.00
1846	31,300	16.00	22.00	35.00	75.00

DIMES

	Quan. Minted	Good	V. Good	Fine	V. Fine
1847	245,000	$3.50	$5.00	$8.00	$15.00
1848	451,500	2.50	3.50	4.50	9.00
1849	839,000	2.25	3.25	4.25	8.00
1849O	300,000	4.50	7.00	10.00	24.00
1850	1,931,500	2.25	3.25	4.25	8.00
1850O	510,000	3.50	5.00	8.00	17.00
1851	1,026,500	2.25	3.25	4.25	8.00
1851O	400,000	3.50	5.00	8.00	17.00
1852	1,535,500	2.25	3.25	4.25	8.00
1852O	430,000	3.50	5.00	8.00	17.00
1853 No arrows at date	95,000	12.00	15.00	22.50	45.00
1853 With arrows	12,078,010	2.75	3.75	5.00	12.00
1853O (Arrows)	1,100,000	3.25	4.25	6.00	13.00
1854 (Arrows)	4,470,000	2.75	3.75	5.00	12.00
1854O (Arrows)	1,770,000	3.25	4.25	6.00	12.00
1855 (Arrows)	2,075,000	2.75	3.75	5.00	12.00
1856	5,780,000	2.25	3.25	4.00	8.00
1856O	1,180,000	2.25	3.50	4.25	8.50
1856S	70,000	16.50	25.00	40.00	70.00
1857	5,580,000	2.25	3.25	4.00	8.00
1857O	1,540,000	2.25	3.25	4.25	8.50
1858	1,540,000	2.25	3.25	4.25	8.00
1858O	290,000	2.50	3.50	4.50	10.00
1858S	60,000	11.00	15.00	26.00	55.00
1859	430,000	2.25	3.25	4.00	8.00
1859 Obv. of 1859. Rev. of 1860					——
1859O	480,000	2.25	3.25	4.25	8.50
1859S	60,000	10.00	15.00	23.00	50.00
1860S (Stars on Obv.)	140,000	5.00	7.50	15.00	32.00

Legend on Obverse 1860-1891

	Quan. Minted	Good	V. Good	Fine	V. Fine
1860 (Legend replaces stars)	607,000	2.25	3.25	4.00	7.00
1860O	40,000	150.00	250.00	350.00	600.00
1861	1,884,000	2.25	3.25	4.00	7.00
1861S	172,500	8.00	11.00	17.00	35.00
1862	847,550	2.25	3.25	4.00	7.00
1862S	180,750	5.00	7.50	12.50	27.50
1863	14,460	22.00	26.00	45.00	70.00
1863S	157,500	5.00	9.00	15.00	30.00
1864	11,470	25.00	30.00	55.00	80.00
1864S	230,000	5.00	7.50	12.50	24.00
1865	10,500	33.00	45.00	65.00	100.00
1865S	175,000	5.00	7.50	12.50	24.00
1866	8,725	33.00	45.00	65.00	95.00
1866S	135,000	5.00	8.00	14.00	26.00
1867	6,625	33.00	45.00	65.00	110.00
1867S	140,000	5.00	8.00	14.00	26.00

DIMES

	Quan. Minted	Good	V. Good	Fine	V. Fine
1868	464,600	$2.25	$3.25	$4.00	$7.00
1868S	260,000	3.75	4.75	6.75	12.00
1869	256,600	2.25	3.25	4.00	7.00
1869S	450,000	3.50	4.50	6.50	12.00
1870	471,500	2.25	3.25	4.00	7.00
1870S	50,000	22.50	32.50	47.50	75.00
1871	907,710	2.25	3.25	4.00	7.00
1871CC	20,100	80.00	125.00	200.00	425.00
1871S	320,000	5.00	7.50	12.50	24.00
1872	2,396,450	2.25	3.25	4.00	7.00
1872CC	35,480	50.00	70.00	110.00	225.00
1872S	190,000	5.50	8.00	12.50	23.00
1873 No arrows	1,568,600	2.25	3.25	4.00	7.00
1873CC No arrows	12,400	Unique			
1873 With arrows	2,378,500	5.50	7.50	12.00	23.00
1873CC With arrows	18,791	200.00	325.00	425.00	675.00
1873S With arrows	455,000	7.50	11.00	16.00	27.00
1874 With arrows	2,940,700	5.50	7.50	12.00	23.00
1874CC With arrows	10,817	95.00	150.00	200.00	400.00
1874S With arrows	240,000	9.00	12.00	20.00	40.00
1875	10,350,700	2.00	2.75	4.00	6.00
1875CC	4,645,000	2.00	2.75	4.00	6.00
1875S	9,070,000	2.00	2.75	4.00	6.00
1876	11,461,150	2.00	2.75	4.00	6.00
1876CC	8,270,000	2.00	2.75	4.00	6.00
1876S	10,420,000	2.00	2.75	4.00	6.00
1877	7,310,510	2.00	2.75	4.00	6.00
1877CC	7,700,000	2.00	2.75	4.00	6.00
1877S	2,340,000	2.00	2.75	4.00	6.00
1878	1,678,800	2.00	2.75	4.00	6.00
1878CC	200,000	7.50	11.00	15.00	24.00
1879	15,100	28.00	35.00	45.00	67.00
1880	37,355	22.00	30.00	40.00	62.00
1881	24,975	24.00	32.00	42.00	65.00
1882	3,911,100	2.00	2.75	4.00	6.00
1883	7,675,712	2.00	2.75	4.00	6.00
1884	3,366,380	2.00	2.75	4.00	6.00
1884S	564,969	5.00	8.00	9.50	20.00
1885	2,533,427	2.00	2.75	4.00	6.00
1885S	43,690	40.00	55.00	75.00	145.00
1886	6,377,570	2.00	2.75	4.00	6.00
1886S	206,524	5.00	8.00	9.50	17.50
1887	11,283,939	2.00	2.75	4.00	6.00
1887S	4,454,450	2.00	2.75	4.00	6.00
1888	5,496,487	2.00	2.75	4.00	6.00
1888S	1,720,000	2.00	2.75	4.00	6.00
1889	7,380,711	2.00	2.75	4.00	6.00
1889S	972,678	4.50	6.50	9.00	25.00
1890	9,911,541	2.00	2.75	4.00	6.00
1890S	1,423,076	2.25	3.00	5.00	7.00
1891	15,310,600	2.00	2.75	4.00	6.00
1891O	4,540,000	2.00	2.75	4.00	10.00
1891S	3,196,116	2.00	2.75	4.00	6.00

DIMES
BARBER OR LIBERTY HEAD TYPE 1892-1916

This type was designed by Charles E. Barber, Chief Engraver of the Mint. His initial B is at the truncation of the neck. He also designed quarters and half dollars of the same period.

GOOD—*Date and letters plain. LIBERTY over brow is obliterated.*
FINE—*All letters in LIBERTY visible though some are weak.*
V. FINE—*All letters of LIBERTY evenly plain.*

	Quan. Minted	Good	Fine	V. Fine
1892	12,121,245	$1.00	$2.50	$5.00
1892O	3,841,700	2.00	5.00	6.50
1892S	990,710	11.00	22.00	35.00
1893	3,340,792	1.75	4.75	6.25
1893O	1,760,000	4.00	10.00	17.00
1893S	2,491,401	3.25	7.00	12.00
1894	1,330,972	3.00	6.00	10.00
1894O	720,000	15.00	40.00	60.00
1894S	24	——	——	——
1895	690,880	15.00	45.00	65.00
1895O	440,000	38.00	85.00	130.00
1895S	1,120,000	7.00	20.00	30.00
1896	2,000,762	3.00	9.00	12.00
1896O	610,000	20.00	45.00	65.00
1896S	575,056	17.00	40.00	55.00
1897	10,869,264	.70	1.85	4.00
1897O	666,000	14.00	35.00	45.00
1897S	1,342,844	4.00	12.00	20.00
1898	16,320,735	.70	1.35	3.50
1898O	2,130,000	2.25	7.00	16.00
1898S	1,702,507	2.00	6.00	12.00
1899	19,580,846	.70	1.35	3.50
1899O	2,650,000	1.75	7.00	15.00
1899S	1,867,493	1.75	6.00	11.00
1900	17,600,912	.70	1.35	3.50
1900O	2,010,000	2.00	7.00	14.00
1900S	5,168,270	1.00	3.50	6.00
1901	18,860,478	.70	1.35	3.50
1901O	5,620,000	.90	3.50	8.50
1901S	593,022	20.00	50.00	85.00
1902	21,380,777	.70	1.35	3.50
1902O	4,500,000	.90	3.50	7.00
1902S	2,070,000	1.75	6.00	12.50
1903	19,500,755	.70	1.35	3.50
1903O	8,180,000	.80	2.50	6.00
1903S	613,300	15.00	28.00	40.00
1904	14,601,027	.70	1.35	3.50
1904S	800,000	12.00	22.00	30.00
1905	14,552,350	.70	1.35	3.50
1905O	3,400,000	.85	4.00	7.00
1905S	6,855,199	.75	2.75	6.00
1906	19,958,406	.70	1.35	3.50
1906D	4,060,000	.80	2.50	4.50

DIMES

	Quan. Minted	Good	Fine	V. Fine
1906O	2,610,000	$1.25	$6.00	$10.00
1906S	3,136,640	1.00	3.25	5.00
1907	22,220,575	.60	1.35	3.00
1907D	4,080,000	.70	2.75	4.50
1907O	5,058,000	.70	2.75	4.50
1907S	3,178,470	.75	3.00	5.00
1908	10,600,545	.60	1.35	3.00
1908D	7,490,000	.60	1.35	3.00
1908O	1,789,000	1.50	5.00	9.00
1908S	3,220,000	.80	2.75	5.00
1909	10,240,650	.60	1.35	3.00
1909D	954,000	1.75	6.50	13.00
1909O	2,287,000	1.00	4.25	7.00
1909S	1,000,000	1.75	7.50	15.00
1910	11,520,551	.60	1.35	3.00
1910D	3,490,000	.70	1.50	4.00
1910S	1,240,000	1.25	4.00	8.00
1911	18,870,543	.60	1.35	3.00
1911D	11,209,000	.60	1.35	3.00
1911S	3,520,000	.70	1.50	4.50
1912	19,350,700	.60	1.35	3.00
1912D	11,760,000	.60	1.35	3.00
1912S	3,420,000	.70	2.25	4.50
1913	19,760,622	.60	1.35	3.00
1913S	510,000	4.00	16.00	27.50
1914	17,360,655	.60	1.35	3.00
1914D	11,908,000	.60	1.35	3.00
1914S	2,100,000	.90	2.25	5.00
1915	5,620,450	.60	1.35	3.00
1915S	960,000	1.00	3.00	6.50
1916 Old type	18,490,000	.60	1.35	3.00
1916S Old type	5,820,000	.60	1.35	3.00

WINGED LIBERTY HEAD or "MERCURY TYPE 1916-1945

Although this coin is often called the "Mercury Dime," the main device is actually a representation of Liberty. The wings crowning her cap are intended to symbolize freedom of thought. The designer A. A. Weinman's monogram AW is at the right of the neck.

GOOD—*Letters and dates clear. Lines and diagonal bands in fasces are obliterated.*

FINE—*All sticks in fasces are defined. Diagonal bands worn at center high points only.*

V. FINE—*Diagonal bands show where they cross fasces.*

1916 New type	22,180,080	.65	1.00	2.00
1916D New type	264,000	125.00	235.00	325.00
1916S New type	10,450,000	.65	1.50	2.75
1917	55,230,000	.60	.70	.80
1917D	9,402,000	1.00	3.00	6.00
1917S	27,330,000	.60	.75	1.35
1918	26,680,000	.60	.80	1.75
1918D	22,674,800	.60	1.50	2.50
1918S	19,300,000	.60	1.25	2.25
1919	35,740,000	.60	.80	1.25

DIMES

	Quan. Minted	Good	Fine	V. Fine
1919D	9,939,000	$ .70	$2.00	$6.00
1919S	8,850,000	.70	2.00	6.00
1920	59,030,000	.60	.70	.85
1920D	19,171,000	.60	.90	2.25
1920S	13,820,000	.60	.90	2.25
1921	1,230,000	9.00	30.00	55.00
1921D	1,080,000	17.00	42.00	80.00
1923	50,130,000	.60	.70	.80
1923S	6,440,000	.75	2.00	3.75
1924	24,010,000	.60	.65	.70
1924D	6,810,000	.60	1.00	2.25
1924S	7,120,000	.60	1.25	2.75
1925	25,610,000	.60	.65	.85
1925D	5,117,000	1.00	3.25	9.50
1925S	5,850,000	.60	1.00	2.50
1926	32,160,000	.60	.65	.70
1926D	6,828,000	.60	1.00	2.25
1926S	1,520,000	4.00	7.50	13.00
1927	28,080,000	.60	.65	.70
1927D	4,812,000	.60	2.25	6.50
1927S	4,770,000	.60	1.25	3.00
1928	19,480,000	.60	.65	.70
1928D	4,161,000	.60	1.75	3.50
1928S	7,400,000	.60	.75	1.75
1929	25,970,000	.60	.65	.70
1929D	5,034,000	.60	.65	.85
1929S	4,730,000	.60	.65	.85
1930	6,770,000	.60	.65	.75
1930S	1,843,000	1.35	1.85	3.00
1931	3,150,000	.60	.85	1.75
1931D	1,260,000	3.00	4.75	8.00
1931S	1,800,000	1.50	2.65	4.25
1934	24,080,000			.60
1934D	6,772,000			.60
1935	58,830,000			.60
1935D	10,477,000			.60
1935S	15,840,000			.60
Proof quantities shown in parentheses				
1936 (4,130)	87,504,130			.60
1936D	16,132,000			.65
1936S	9,210,000			.60
1937 (5,756)	56,865,756			.60
1937D	14,146,000			.60
1937S	9,740,000			.60
1938 (8,728)	22,198,728			.60
1938D	5,537,000			.60
1938S	8,090,000			.60
1939 (9,321)	67,749,321			.60
1939D	24,394,000			.60
1939S	10,540,000			.60
1940 (11,827)	65,361,827			.60
1940D	21,198,000			.60
1940S	21,560,000			.60

DIMES

	Quan. Minted	V. Good	Fine	V. Fine
1941 (16,557)	175,106,557			$ .60
1941D	45,634,000			.60
1941S	43,090,000			.60
1942 Normal date (22,329)	205,432,329			.60
1942 2 over 1 (Error, see picture p. 12)		$120.00	$140.00	160.00
1942D	60,740,000			.60
1942D 2 over 1		110.00	125.00	180.00
1942S	49,300,000			.60
1943	191,710,000			.60
1943D	71,949,000			.60
1943S	60,400,000			.60
1944	231,410,000			.60
1944D	62,224,000			.60
1944S	49,490,000			.60
1945	159,130,000			.60
1945D	40,245,000			.60
1945S	41,920,000			.60

ROOSEVELT TYPE 1946 to Date

John R. Sinnock (initials JS at the truncation of the neck) designed this coin showing a portrait of Franklin D. Roosevelt. The design has a more modernistic character than preceding types.

FINE—*Torch flame smooth. Vertical lines in torch show, horizontal lines smooth.*

V. FINE—*All vertical lines on torch will show.*

> Common silver coins vary in value according to the prevailing price of silver.

	Quan. Minted	V.F.
1946	255,250,000	$ .60
1946D	61,043,500	.60
1946S	27,900,000	.60
1947	121,520,000	.60
1947D	46,835,000	.60
1947S	34,840,000	.60
1948	74,950,000	.60
1948D	52,841,000	.60
1948S	35,520,000	.60
1949	30,940,000	.60
1949D	26,034,000	.60
1949S	13,510,000	.75

	Quan. Minted	V.F.
1950 (51,386)	50,181,500	$ .60
1950D	46,803,000	.60
1950S	20,440,000	.60
1951 (57,500)	103,937,602	.60
1951D	56,529,000	.60
1951S	31,630,000	.60
1952 (81,980)	99,122,073	.60
1952D	122,100,000	.60
1952S	44,419,500	.60
1953 (128,800)	53,618,920	.60
1953D	136,433,000	.60
1953S	39,180,000	.60
1954 (233,300)	114,243,503	.60
1954D	106,397,000	.60
1954S	22,860,000	.60
1955 (378,200)	12,828,381	.70
1955D	13,959,000	.60
1955S	18,510,000	.60

Dimes prior to 1956 command a premium if in bright uncirculated condition.

ROOSEVELT DIMES

	Quan. Minted	V.F.
1956 (669,384)	109,309,384	$ .60
1956D	108,015,100	.60
1957 (1,247,952)	161,407,952	.60
1957D	113,354,330	.60
1958 (875,652)	32,785,652	.60
1958D	136,564,600	.60
1959 (1,149,291)	86,929,291	.60
1959D	164,919,790	.60
1960 (1,691,602)	72,081,602	.60
1960D	200,160,400	.60
1961 (3,028,244)	96,758,244	.60
1961D	209,146,550	.60
1962 (3,218,019)	75,668,019	.60
1962D	334,948,380	.60
1963 (3,075,645)	126,725,645	.60
1963D	421,476,530	.60
1964 (3,950,762)	933,310,762	.60
1964D	1,357,517,180	.60

CLAD COINAGE

	Quan. Minted	V.F.
1965	1,652,140,570	.10
1966	1,382,734,540	.10
1967	2,244,007,320	.10
1968	424,470,400	.10
1968D	480,748,280	.10
1968S Proof only	(3,041,506)	.40
1969	145,790,000	.10
1969D	563,323,870	.10
1969S Proof only	(2,934,631)	.40

	Quan. Minted	V.F.
1970	345,570,000	$ .10
1970D	754,942,100	.10
1970S Proof only	(2,632,810)	.65
1971	162,690,000	.10
1971D	377,914,240	.10
1971S Proof only	(3,220,733)	.30
1972	431,540,000	.10
1972D	330,290,000	.10
1972S Proof only	(3,260,996)	.30
1973	315,670,000	.10
1973D	455,032,426	.10
1973S Proof only	(2,760,399)	.65
1974	470,248,000	.10
1974D	571,083,000	.10
1974S Proof only	(2,612,568)	.70
1975	585,673,900	.10
1975D	313,705,300	.10
1975S Proof only	(2,845,450)	1.10
1976	568,760,000	.10
1976D	695,222,774	.10
1976S Proof only	(4,149,730)	.55
1977	796,930,000	.10
1977D	376,607,228	.10
1977S Proof only	(3,251,152)	1.10
1978	663,980,000	.10
1978D	282,847,540	.10
1978S Proof only	(3,127,781)	.60
1979		.10
1979D		.10
1979S Proof only		.60

TWENTY-CENT PIECES

(Coined from 1875 to 1878)

This series was a short-lived coinage experiment; soon after the release of these coins the populace complained about their similarity in design and size to the quarter. The 1876CC mint piece is a great rarity, with only about ten known to exist. 1877 and 1878 were struck in proof only.

GOOD—*LIBERTY on shield obliterated. Letters and date legible.*

V. GOOD—*At least 2 letters of LIBERTY show.*

FINE—*At least 3 letters of LIBERTY show.*

V. FINE—*All letters of LIBERTY readable.*

	Quan. Minted	Good	V. Good	Fine	V. Fine
1875	39,700	$31.00	$35.00	$52.00	$70.00
1875CC	133,290	31.00	35.00	52.00	70.00
1875S	1,155,000	27.50	31.00	39.00	60.00
1876	15,900	37.50	45.00	57.00	85.00
1876CC (Only about 10 known)	10,000				
1877 Proofs only	510			Proof	900.00
1878 Proofs only	600			Proof	850.00

QUARTER DOLLARS
Issued from 1796 to date

The first date, 1796, follows the pattern of the early half dimes and dimes by the absence of a mark of value. In 1804 a "25 C." was added to the reverse. This was used until 1838 when QUAR. DOL. appeared although there was sufficient room for a complete spelling of the denomination. It was not until the adoption of the Barber type that the value is spelled out entirely.

DRAPED BUST TYPE, SMALL EAGLE REVERSE 1796

FAIR—*Details clear enough to identify.*

GOOD—*Date readable. Bust outlined, but no detail.*

V. GOOD—*All but deepest drapery folds worn smooth. Hairlines nearly gone and curls lack detail.*

FINE—*All drapery lines visible. Hair partly worn.*

V. FINE—*Only left side of drapery is indistinct.*

	Quan. Minted	Fair	Good	V. Good	Fine	V. Fine
1796	6,146	$475.00	$1,000	$1,400	$2,200	$3,250

DRAPED BUST TYPE, HERALDIC EAGLE REVERSE 1804-1807

	Quan. Minted	Fair	Good	V. Good	Fine	V. Fine
1804	6,738	90.00	130.00	185.00	315.00	625.00
1805	121,394	35.00	60.00	80.00	135.00	275.00
1806	206,124	33.00	55.00	70.00	120.00	230.00
1807	220,643	33.00	55.00	70.00	120.00	230.00

CAPPED BUST TYPE 1815-1838
Variety 1 — Large size, motto above eagle 1815-1828

FAIR—*Details clear enough to identify.*

GOOD—*Date, letters and stars readable. Hair under headband smooth. Cap lines worn smooth.*

V. GOOD—*Rim well defined. Main details visible. Full LIBERTY on cap. Hair above eye nearly smooth.*

FINE—*All hairlines show but drapery has only part details. Shoulder clasp distinct.*

V. FINE—*All details show, but some wear. Clasp and ear sharp.*

QUARTER DOLLARS

	Quan. Minted	Fair	Good	V. Good	Fine	V. Fine
1815	89,235	$13.00	$20.00	$26.00	$48.00	$130.00
1818	361,174	12.00	18.00	24.00	45.00	110.00
1819	144,000	12.00	18.00	24.00	45.00	110.00
1820	127,444	12.00	18.00	24.00	45.00	110.00
1821	216,851	12.00	18.00	24.00	45.00	110.00
1822 Rev. 25 over 50 } 64,080		80.00	95.00	140.00	220.00	400.00
Normal rev.		12.00	18.00	24.00	45.00	110.00
1823 All 3 over 2	17,800	400.00	700.00	1,000	1,600	3,500
1824	———	16.00	22.00	32.00	70.00	120.00
1825	168,000	12.00	18.00	24.00	45.00	100.00
1827 Originals (Rare)	4,000					——
Restrikes (Rare)						——
1828	102,000	12.00	18.00	24.00	45.00	100.00

Variety 2 — Reduced size, no motto 1831-1838

GOOD—*Bust is well defined. Hair under headband is smooth. Date, letters, stars readable. Scant rims.*

V. GOOD—*Details apparent but worn on high spots. Rim strong. Full LIBERTY.*

FINE—*All hairlines visible. Drapery partly worn. Shoulder clasp distinct.*

V. FINE—*Only top spots worn. Clasp sharp. Ear distinct.*

	Quan. Minted	Good	V. Good	Fine	V. Fine
1831	398,000	$21.00	$25.00	$32.00	$55.00
1832	320,000	21.00	25.00	32.00	55.00
1833	156,000	22.00	27.00	35.00	65.00
1834	286,000	21.00	25.00	32.00	55.00
1835	1,952,000	21.00	25.00	32.00	55.00
1836	472,000	21.00	25.00	32.00	55.00
1837	252,400	21.00	25.00	32.00	55.00
1838	Both types 832,000	21.00	25.00	32.00	55.00

LIBERTY SEATED TYPE 1838-1891
Variety 1 — No motto above eagle 1838-1853

GOOD—*Scant rim. LIBERTY on shield worn off. Date and letters readable.*

V. GOOD—*Rim fairly defined, at least 3 letters in LIBERTY evident.*

FINE—*Liberty complete, but partly weak.*

V. FINE—*LIBERTY strong.*

1838 Liberty seated	5.50	7.00	11.00	24.00
1839	491,146	5.50	7.00	11.00	24.00
1840O	All kinds 425,200	5.50	7.00	11.00	24.00

QUARTER DOLLARS

	Quan. Minted	Good	V. Good	Fine	V. Fine
1840 Drapery to elbow	188,127	$5.00	$6.00	$10.00	$22.00
1840O Drapery to elbow		5.00	6.00	10.00	22.00
1841	120,000	8.00	11.00	15.00	24.00
1841O	452,000	4.50	6.00	10.00	26.00
1842	88,000	12.00	25.00	35.00	60.00
1842O	769,000	4.50	6.00	8.00	14.50
1843	645,600	4.50	6.00	8.00	14.50
1843O	968,000	5.00	7.00	10.00	17.00
1844	421,200	4.50	6.00	8.00	14.50
1844O	740,000	4.50	6.00	8.00	14.50
1845	922,000	4.50	6.00	8.00	14.50
1846	510,000	4.50	6.00	8.00	14.50
1847	734,000	4.50	6.00	8.00	14.50
1847O	368,000	4.50	6.00	8.00	14.50
1848	146,000	7.00	10.00	15.00	25.00
1849	340,000	4.50	6.00	8.00	14.50
1849O	——	65.00	90.00	165.00	235.00
1850	190,800	4.50	6.00	8.00	14.50
1850O	412,000	4.50	6.00	9.00	16.00
1851	160,000	4.50	6.00	8.00	14.50
1851O	88,000	25.00	40.00	65.00	125.00
1852	177,060	4.50	6.00	9.00	16.00
1852O	96,000	65.00	100.00	165.00	260.00
1853 Recut date, no arrows and rays (Beware altered 1858)	44,200	45.00	65.00	100.00	150.00

Variety 2 — Arrows at date, rays around eagle 1853 only

1853 Arrows and rays	15,210,020	6.00	7.00	9.00	20.00
1853O Arrows and rays	1,332,000	6.50	8.00	11.00	22.00

Variety 3 — Arrows at date, no rays 1854-1855

1854	12,380,000	4.50	5.50	7.50	14.00
1854O	1,484,000	5.00	6.00	8.00	17.00
1855	2,857,000	5.00	6.00	8.00	17.00
1855O	176,000	25.00	35.00	50.00	100.00
1855S	396,400	25.00	35.00	50.00	90.00

Variety 1 resumed 1856-1865

1856	7,264,000	4.00	5.00	6.50	10.00
1856O	968,000	4.00	5.50	7.00	12.00
1856S	286,000	12.00	17.50	25.00	55.00

QUARTER DOLLARS

	Quan. Minted	Good	V. Good	Fine	V. Fine
1857	9,644,000	$4.00	$5.00	$6.50	$10.00
1857O	1,180,000	4.00	5.50	7.00	12.00
1857S	82,000	15.00	24.00	35.00	65.00
1858	7,368,000	4.00	5.00	6.50	10.00
1858O	520,000	4.00	5.50	7.00	12.00
1858S	121,000	15.00	22.00	30.00	57.50
1859	1,344,000	4.00	5.00	6.50	10.00
1859O	260,000	4.50	6.00	9.00	15.00
1859S	80,000	18.00	27.50	45.00	75.00
1860	805,400	4.00	5.00	6.50	10.00
1860O	388,000	4.50	6.00	9.00	15.00
1860S	56,000	20.00	30.00	50.00	90.00
1861	4,854,600	4.00	5.00	6.50	10.00
1861S	96,000	13.50	17.00	25.00	50.00
1862	932,550	4.00	5.00	6.50	10.00
1862S	67,000	14.00	18.00	27.50	57.50
1863	192,060	6.00	9.00	13.00	19.00
1864	94,070	12.00	15.00	25.00	40.00
1864S	20,000	42.50	80.00	110.00	175.00
1865	59,300	15.00	20.00	30.00	50.00
1865S	41,000	15.00	20.00	30.00	60.00

**Variety 4 —
Motto above eagle
1866-1873**

	Quan. Minted	Good	V. Good	Fine	V. Fine
1866 With motto — (In God We Trust)	17,525	24.00	30.00	47.50	90.00
1866S With motto	28,000	16.00	22.50	37.50	70.00
1867	20,625	17.00	25.00	40.00	80.00
1867S	48,000	14.00	19.00	30.00	55.00
1868	30,000	12.00	17.00	28.00	55.00
1868S	96,000	12.00	17.00	28.00	50.00
1869	16,600	22.00	27.50	45.00	80.00
1869S	76,000	12.00	17.00	28.00	50.00
1870	87,400	10.00	15.00	25.00	35.00
1870CC	8,340	175.00	230.00	350.00	550.00
1871	119,160	4.50	5.50	8.50	14.00
1871CC	10,890	110.00	160.00	260.00	425.00
1871S	30,900	24.00	50.00	80.00	125.00
1872	182,950	4.00	5.00	6.50	10.00
1872CC	22,850	100.00	125.00	175.00	315.00
1872S	83,000	30.00	55.00	90.00	160.00
1873 Without arrows	212,600	4.00	5.00	6.50	10.00
1873CC Without arrows	4,000				——

Variety 5 — Arrows at date 1873-1874

	Quan. Minted	Good	V. Good	Fine	V. Fine
1873 Arrows	1,271,700	9.00	13.00	17.00	37.50

QUARTER DOLLARS

	Quan. Minted	Good	V. Good	Fine	V. Fine
1873CC Arrows	12,462	$200.00	$275.00	$400.00	$625.00
1873S Arrows	156,000	11.00	15.00	20.00	42.50
1874 Arrows	471,900	9.00	13.00	17.00	37.50
1874S Arrows	392,000	11.00	15.00	20.00	42.50

Variety 4 resumed 1875-1891

	Quan. Minted	Good	V. Good	Fine	V. Fine
1875	4,293,500	4.00	4.75	6.00	10.00
1875CC	140,000	10.00	15.00	25.00	45.00
1875S	680,000	5.50	7.00	12.00	20.00
1876	17,817,150	4.00	4.75	6.00	10.00
1876CC	4,944,000	4.00	5.00	6.50	14.00
1876S	8,596,000	4.00	4.75	6.00	10.00
1877	10,911,710	4.00	4.75	6.00	10.00
1877CC	4,192,000	4.00	5.00	6.50	14.00
1877S	8,996,000	4.00	4.75	6.00	10.00
1878	2,260,800	4.00	4.75	6.00	10.00
1878CC	996,000	5.00	6.00	8.00	14.00
1878S	140,000	35.00	50.00	70.00	100.00
1879	14,700	25.00	33.00	45.00	70.00
1880	14,955	25.00	33.00	45.00	70.00
1881	12,975	25.00	33.00	45.00	70.00
1882	16,300	24.00	31.50	42.50	65.00
1883	15,439	24.00	31.50	42.50	65.00
1884	8,875	32.50	42.50	55.00	80.00
1885	14,530	24.00	31.50	42.50	65.00
1886	5,886	37.50	50.00	65.00	90.00
1887	10,710	35.00	44.00	52.50	80.00
1888	10,833	35.00	44.00	52.50	80.00
1888S	1,216,000	4.00	4.75	6.50	12.00
1889	12,711	25.00	33.00	45.00	75.00
1890	80,590	15.00	20.00	27.50	35.00
1891	3,920,600	4.00	4.75	6.50	12.00
1891O	68,000	50.00	65.00	90.00	140.00
(Only date of this type struck at New Orleans Mint.)					
1891S	2,216,000	4.50	5.25	7.00	12.00

BARBER or LIBERTY HEAD TYPE 1892-1916

GOOD—*Date and legends readable. LIBERTY worn off of headband.*

V. GOOD—*Minimum of 3 letters in LIBERTY readable.*

FINE—*LIBERTY completely readable but not sharp.*

V. FINE—*All letters in LIBERTY evenly plain.*

1892	8,237,245	1.50	1.75	4.00	12.00
1892O	2,640,000	2.25	3.25	6.00	15.00
1892S	964,079	7.00	11.00	17.00	27.00
1893	5,444,815	1.50	1.75	4.00	12.00
1893O	3,396,000	1.75	3.25	6.00	14.00
1893S	1,454,535	3.00	5.00	10.00	20.00
1894	3,432,972	1.50	1.75	4.00	12.00

QUARTER DOLLARS

	Quan. Minted	Good	V. Good	Fine	V. Fine
1894O	2,852,000	$1.50	$3.25	$6.00	$13.00
1894S	2,648,821	1.50	3.25	6.00	13.00
1895	4,440,880	1.50	1.75	3.25	11.00
1895O	2,816,000	1.50	3.25	6.00	13.00
1895S	1,764,681	2.50	4.00	7.00	16.00
1896	3,874,762	1.50	1.75	3.25	11.00
1896O	1,484,000	2.50	4.00	10.00	20.00
1896S	188,039	90.00	125.00	200.00	275.00
1897	8,140,731	1.50	1.75	3.25	11.00
1897O	1,414,800	3.00	5.00	9.00	20.00
1897S	542,229	6.00	8.75	15.00	25.00
1898	11,100,735	1.50	1.75	3.50	12.00
1898O	1,868,000	2.00	4.00	7.00	16.00
1898S	1,020,592	2.50	4.00	7.00	16.00
1899	12,624,846	1.50	1.75	3.25	11.00
1899O	2,644,000	1.75	2.00	6.00	14.00
1899S	708,000	4.00	6.50	10.00	18.00
1900	10,016,912	1.50	1.75	3.25	11.00
1900O	3,416,000	2.00	4.00	7.00	16.00
1900S	1,858,585	1.50	2.00	4.50	13.00
1901	8,892,813	1.50	1.75	3.25	11.00
1901O	1,612,000	5.00	9.00	19.00	36.00
1901S	72,664	315.00	400.00	475.00	625.00
1902	12,197,744	1.50	1.75	3.25	11.00
1902O	4,748,000	1.75	2.00	4.50	12.50
1902S	1,524,612	3.50	6.00	10.00	17.50
1903	9,670,064	1.50	1.75	3.50	12.00
1903O	3,500,000	1.50	2.50	5.50	15.00
1903S	1,036,000	3.50	5.00	9.00	20.00
1904	9,588,813	1.50	1.75	3.25	11.00
1904O	2,456,000	2.50	4.25	8.50	18.00
1905	4,968,250	1.50	1.75	3.25	11.00
1905O	1,230,000	2.75	5.00	8.75	19.00
1905S	1,884,000	2.00	3.00	5.50	13.00
1906	3,656,435	1.50	1.75	3.25	11.00
1906D	3,280,000	1.50	1.75	4.00	14.00
1906O	2,056,000	1.75	2.75	4.50	15.00
1907	7,192,575	1.50	1.75	3.25	11.00
1907D	2,484,000	1.50	1.75	3.25	11.00
1907O	4,560,000	1.50	1.75	3.25	11.00
1907S	1,360,000	1.50	2.00	3.50	12.00
1908	4,232,545	1.50	1.75	3.25	11.00
1908D	5,788,000	1.50	1.75	3.25	11.00
1908O	6,244,000	1.50	1.75	3.25	11.00
1908S	784,000	3.25	5.50	9.00	15.00
1909	9,268,650	1.50	1.75	3.25	11.00
1909D	5,114,000	1.50	1.75	3.25	11.00
1909O	712,000	6.00	9.50	19.00	35.00
1909S	1,348,000	1.50	2.00	3.50	11.00
1910	2,244,551	1.50	1.75	3.25	11.00
1910D	1,500,000	1.50	2.00	3.50	11.00
1911	3,720,543	1.50	1.75	3.25	11.00
1911D	933,600	1.50	2.25	5.50	14.00
1911S	988,000	1.50	2.25	5.50	14.00

QUARTER DOLLARS

	Quan. Minted	Good	V. Good	Fine	V. Fine
1912	4,400,700	$1.50	$1.75	$3.25	$11.00
1912S	708,000	1.50	2.25	5.50	15.00
1913	484,613	4.00	7.00	16.00	40.00
1913D	1,450,800	1.75	2.50	5.00	14.00
1913S	40,000	110.00	140.00	250.00	350.00
1914	6,244,610	1.50	1.75	3.25	11.00
1914D	3,046,000	1.50	1.75	3.25	11.00
1914S	264,000	6.00	10.00	17.00	40.00
1915	3,480,450	1.50	1.75	3.25	11.00
1915D	3,694,000	1.50	1.75	3.25	11.00
1915S	704,000	1.50	2.25	5.50	15.00
1916	1,788,000	1.50	1.75	3.25	11.00
1916D	6,540,800	1.50	1.75	3.25	11.00

STANDING LIBERTY TYPE 1916-1930

This design is by Hermon A. MacNeil, whose initial M is above and to the right of the date. Liberty bears a shield of protection in her left arm, while the right hand holds the olive branch of peace. There was a modification in 1917. The reverse has a new arrangement of stars and the eagle is higher.

Variety 1 — No stars below eagle 1916-1917

GOOD—Date and lettering readable. Top of date worn. Liberty's right leg and toes worn off.

V. GOOD—Distinct date. Toes show faintly. Drapery lines visible above her left leg.

FINE—High curve of right leg flat from thigh to ankle.

V. FINE—Garment line worn but shows at sides.

(Some modifications must be made for grading variety 2.)

1916	52,000	250.00	350.00	450.00	600.00
1917	8,740,000	4.00	5.00	8.00	15.00
1917D	1,509,200	5.00	6.00	9.00	18.00
1917S	1,952,000	5.00	6.00	9.00	18.00

Variety 2 — Stars below eagle 1917-1930

1917	13,880,000	3.50	4.00	5.75	10.00
1917D	6,224,400	5.00	7.00	10.00	18.00
1917S	5,552,000	5.75	7.50	11.00	19.00
1918	14,240,000	4.00	4.50	6.00	11.00
1918D	7,380,000	5.00	7.00	10.00	16.00
1918S Normal date } 1918S 8 over 7 (See page 11) }	11,072,000	4.00 / 150.00	5.00 / 250.00	6.50 / 400.00	12.00 / 600.00
1919	11,324,000	4.00	5.00	6.50	13.00
1919D	1,944,000	19.00	24.00	35.00	45.00
1919S	1,836,000	19.00	24.00	35.00	50.00
1920	27,860,000	3.50	4.00	6.00	8.50

QUARTER DOLLARS

	Quan. Minted	Good	V. Good	Fine	V. Fine
1920D	3,586,400	$7.00	$10.00	$12.00	$20.00
1920S	6,380,000	4.50	6.00	8.00	12.00
1921	1,916,000	19.00	24.00	35.00	50.00
1923	9,716,000	3.50	4.50	6.00	8.00
1923S*	1,360,000	30.00	37.00	52.00	70.00
1924	10,920,000	3.00	4.00	6.00	8.00
1924D	3,112,000	6.50	9.00	12.00	20.00
1924S	2,860,000	5.00	7.00	9.50	15.00

*Beware altered date.

Liberty standing quarters minted from 1916 to 1924 are scarce in any condition. The quarters struck during this period had the date in the same position as later issues, but because that part of the coin was high it received much wear and after a few years in circulation became obliterated. After 1924 the date was "recessed," thereby permitting coin to wear and date remain legible.

	Quan. Minted	Good	V. Good	Fine	V. Fine
1925	12,280,000	1.50	1.60	1.75	5.50
1926	11,316,000	1.50	1.60	1.75	5.50
1926D	1,716,000	1.50	1.60	2.75	6.50
1926S	2,700,000	1.75	2.00	3.00	8.75
1927	11,912,000	1.50	1.60	1.75	5.50
1927D	976,400	1.75	2.25	4.50	10.00
1927S	396,000	3.00	4.00	8.00	30.00
1928	6,336,000	1.50	1.60	1.75	5.50
1928D	1,627,600	1.50	1.60	1.75	5.50
1928S	2,644,000	1.50	1.60	1.75	5.50
1929	11,140,000	1.50	1.60	1.75	5.50
1929D	1,358,000	1.50	1.60	2.75	6.50
1929S	1,764,000	1.50	1.60	1.75	5.50
1930	5,632,000	1.50	1.60	1.75	5.50
1930S	1,556,000	1.50	1.60	1.75	5.50

WASHINGTON TYPE 1932 to 1974

This coin was intended to commemorate the bicentennial of the birth of George Washington. The designer was John Flanagan; his initials JF are found at the base of the neck.

Variety 1 — Silver 1932-1964

Quarters dated prior to 1956 command a premium if in bright uncirculated condition.

GOOD—Letters and date flat, but separated from rim. No hairlines near face.

V. GOOD—Wing-tips outlined. Rims on both sides are fine and even. Tops of letters at rim are flattened.

FINE—Hairlines about ear are visible. Tiny feathers on eagle's breast are faintly visible.

V. FINE—Hair details worn but plain. Feathers at sides of eagle's breast are plain.

	Quan. Minted	Good	V. Good	Fine	V. Fine
1932	5,404,000	1.35	1.35	1.35	1.50
1932D	436,800	26.00	29.00	33.00	43.00
1932S	408,000	25.00	28.00	31.00	36.00
1934	31,912,052	1.35	1.35	1.35	1.50
1934D	3,527,200	1.60	1.70	1.80	2.60

QUARTER DOLLARS

	Quan. Minted	Good	V. Good	Fine	V. Fine
1935 32,484,000		$ 1.35	$ 1.35	$ 1.35	$ 1.50
1935D.......................... 5,780,000		1.50	1.60	1.85	2.00
1935S.......................... 5,660,000		1.50	1.60	1.85	2.00
1936 (3,837) .... 6.50 ... 41,303,837		1.35	1.35	1.35	1.35
1936D.......................... 5,374,000		1.50	1.60	1.85	5.00
1936S.......................... 3,828,000		1.35	1.35	1.35	1.50
1937 (5,542) 19,701,542		1.35	1.35	1.35	1.35
1937D.......................... 7,189,600		1.50	1.60	1.75	1.85
1937S.......................... 1,652,000		2.00	2.20	3.00	4.25
1938 (8,045) 9,480,045		1.35	1.35	1.35	1.50
1938S.......................... 2,832,000		1.35	1.35	1.50	2.00
1939 (8,795) 33,548,795		1.35	1.35	1.35	1.50
1939D.......................... 7,092,000		1.50	1.60	1.75	1.85
1939S.......................... 2,628,000		1.60	1.70	2.00	2.10
1940 (11,246) 35,715,246		1.35	1.35	1.35	1.35
1940D.......................... 2,797,600		1.60	1.70	2.00	2.10
1940S.......................... 8,244,000		1.35	1.35	1.35	1.35

	Quan. Minted	Fine	V. Fine
1941 (15,287) 79,047,287		1.35	1.35
1941D... 16,714,800		1.35	1.35
1941S... 16,080,000		1.35	1.35
1942 (21,123) 102,117,123		1.35	1.35
1942D... 17,487,200		1.35	1.35
1942S... 19,384,000		1.35	1.50
1943 99,700,000		1.35	1.35
1943D... 16,095,600		1.35	1.35
1943S... 21,700,000		1.35	1.35
1944 104,956,000		1.35	1.35
1944D... 14,600,800		1.35	1.35
1944S 12,560,000		1.35	1.35
1945 74,372,000		1.35	1.35
1945D...... 12,341,600		1.35	1.35
1945S...... 17,004,001		1.35	1.35
1946 53,436,000		1.35	1.35
1946D... 9,072,800		1.35	1.35
1946S... 4,204,000		1.50	1.75
1947 22,556,000		1.35	1.35
1947D... 15,338,400		1.35	1.35
1947S... 5,532,000		1.35	1.35
1948 35,196,000		1.35	1.35
1948D... 16,766,800		1.35	1.35
1948S... 15,960,000		1.35	1.35
1949 9,312,000		1.35	1.50
1949D... 10,068,400		1.35	1.35
1950 (51,386) 24,971,512		1.35	1.35
1950D... 21,075,600		1.35	1.35
1950S... 10,284,004		1.35	1.35
1951 (57,500) 43,505,602		1.35	1.35
1951D... 35,354,800		1.35	1.35
1951S... 9,048,000		1.35	1.35
1952 (81,980) 38,862,073		1.35	1.35
1952D... 49,795,200		1.35	1.35
1952S... 13,707,800		1.35	1.35

> **Common silver coins vary in value according to the prevailing price of silver.**

QUARTER DOLLARS

	Quan. Minted	Fine	V. Fine
1953 (128,800)	18,664,920	$ 1.35	$ 1.35
1953D	56,112,400	1.35	1.35
1953S	14,016,000	1.35	1.35
1954 (233,300)	54,645,503	1.35	1.35
1954D	46,305,500	1.35	1.35
1954S	11,834,722	1.35	1.35
1955 (378,200)	18,558,381	1.35	1.35
1955D	3,182,400	1.50	1.75
1956 (669,384)	44,813,384	1.35	1.35
1956D	32,334,500	1.35	1.35
1957 (1,247,952)	47,779,952	1.35	1.35
1957D	77,924,160	1.35	1.35
1958 (875,652)	7,235,652	1.50	1.60
1958D	78,124,900	1.35	1.35
1959 (1,149,291)	25,533,291	1.35	1.35
1959D	62,054,232	1.35	1.35
1960 (1,691,602)	30,855,602	1.35	1.35
1960D	63,000,324	1.35	1.35
1961 (3,028,244)	40,064,244	1.35	1.35
1961D	83,656,928	1.35	1.35
1962 (3,218,019)	39,374,019	1.35	1.35
1962D	127,554,756	1.35	1.35
1963 (3,075,645)	77,391,645	1.35	1.35
1963D	135,288,184	1.35	1.35
1964 (3,950,762)	564,341,347	1.35	1.35
1964D	704,135,528	1.35	1.35

CLAD COINAGE
Variety 2 — Clad copper-nickel 1965 to Date

	Quan. Minted	Unc.		Quan. Minted	Unc.
1965	1,819,717,540	$ .25	1972D	311,067,732	$ .25
1966	821,101,500	.25	1972S Proof only	(3,260,996)	.45
1967	1,524,031,848	.25	1973	346,924,000	.25
1968	220,731,500	.25	1973D	232,977,400	.25
1968D	101,534,000	.25	1973S Proof only	(2,760,339)	.85
1968S Proof only	(3,041,506)	.50	1974	801,456,000	.25
1969	176,212,000	.25	1974D	353,160,300	.25
1969D	114,372,000	.25	1974S Proof only	(2,612,568)	.85
1969S Proof only	(2,934,631)	.50	1977	468,556,000	.25
1970	136,420,000	.25	1977D	256,524,978	.25
1970D	417,341,364	.25	1977S Proof only	(3,251,152)	.65
1970S Proof only	(2,632,810)	.85	1978	521,452,000	.25
1971	109,284,000	.25	1978D	287,373,152	.25
1971D	258,634,428	.25	1978S Proof only	(3,127,781)	.80
1971S Proof only	(3,220,733)	.45	1979		.25
1972	215,048,000	.25	1979D		.25
			1979S Proof only		.80

BICENTENNIAL COINAGE DATED 1776-1976

One of the most momentous holidays of the United States was the Bicentennial of its founding. In 1973, the Treasury announced an open contest for the selection of suitable reverse designs for the quarter, half dollar and dollar. A prize of $5,000 was to be awarded to each winner. Out of twelve semifinalists, the symbolic entry of Jack L. Ahr was chosen for the quarter. It features a

QUARTER DOLLARS

Colonial drummer with a victory torch encircled by thirteen stars. Except for the dual dating 1776-1976 the obverse remains unchanged. Pieces with this dating were coined during 1975 and 1976, for general circulation as well as special proof and mint sets. Collectors' issued include a quarter in clad silver which until 1975 had never been made.

	Quan. Minted	Unc.	Proof
1976 Copper-nickel clad	809,784,016	$ .25	
1976D Copper-nickel clad	860,118,839	.25	
1976S Copper-nickel clad (Proof only)	(7,059,099)		$ .65
1976S Silver Clad	(*4,000,000) *11,000,000	1.00	2.00

*Approximate mintage. Not all released

HALF DOLLARS

(Coined from 1794 to date)

Half dollars comprise a series that has been extensively collected by "varieties," and many dates cointain both rare and common varieties. The collector who cares to go into the study of half dollar varieties should obtain a copy of Beistle's work on half dollars or a more recent book, *Early Half Dollar Varieties 1794-1836* by Al C. Overton.

Half dollars between about 1812 and 1840 are more or less common in ordinary circulated condition. This might be explained by the fact that the U.S. government did not issue silver dollars during this period. The half thus became the "big" silver money and coinage was plentiful according to standards of the time.

FLOWING HAIR TYPE 1794-1795

FAIR—*Clear enough to identify.*

GOOD—*Date and letters sufficient to be readable. Main devices outlined, but lack details.*

V. GOOD—*Major details discernible. Letters well formed but worn.*

FINE—*Hair ends distinguishable. Top hairlines show, but otherwise worn smooth.*

V. FINE—*Hair in center shows some detail. Other details more bold.*

	Quan. Minted	Fair	Good	V. Good	Fine	V. Fine
1794	23,464	$125.00	$235.00	$350.00	$475.00	$900.00
1795 All kinds	299,680					
Re-engraved date, 3 leaves under wings		120.00	225.00	325.00	450.00	875.00
Perfect date, 2 leaves under wings		100.00	175.00	225.00	350.00	500.00

HALF DOLLARS
DRAPED BUST TYPE, SMALL EAGLE REVERSE 1796-1797

Grading same as above for Fair to Fine

V. FINE—Right side of drapery slightly worn. Left side to curls is smooth.

	Quan. Minted	Fair	Good	V. Good	Fine	V. Fine
1796 15 stars	⎫	$1,000	$2,000	$3,000	$4,250	$6,000
16 stars	⎬ 3,918	1,000	2,000	3,000	4,250	6,000
1797	⎭	1,000	2,000	3,000	4,250	6,000

DRAPED BUST TYPE, HERALDIC EAGLE REVERSE 1801-1807

GOOD—Letters and date readable. E. PLURIBUS UNUM obliterated.

V. GOOD—Motto partially readable. Only deepest drapery details visible. All other lines smooth.

FINE—All drapery lines distinguishable. Hairlines near cheek and neck show some detail.

V. FINE—Left side of drapery worn smooth.

	Quan. Minted	Good	V. Good	Fine	V. Fine
1801	30,289	$62.00	$80.00	$160.00	$275.00
1802	29,890	55.00	75.00	125.00	225.00
1803	188,234	35.00	45.00	70.00	125.00
1805 5 over 4	⎫ 211,722	42.50	55.00	85.00	150.00
Normal date	⎭	30.00	35.00	55.00	95.00
1806 6 over 5	⎫	32.50	40.00	60.00	110.00
6 over inverted 6	⎬ 839,576	37.50	50.00	100.00	135.00
Normal date	⎭	22.50	30.00	45.00	75.00
1807	301,076	22.50	30.00	45.00	75.00

CAPPED BUST TYPE 1807-1839

[64]

HALF DOLLARS

Variety 1 — Lettered edge 1807-1836

	Quan. Minted	Good	V. Good	Fine	V. Fine
1807 Face to left..................	750,500	$15.00	$17.00	$22.00	$40.00
1808 8 over 7.................. }	1,368,600	12.00	14.00	20.00	25.00
1808 Normal date.............. }		11.00	13.00	20.00	25.00
1809	1,405,810	11.00	13.00	16.00	22.00
1810	1,276,276	11.00	13.00	16.00	22.00
1811	1,203,644	10.00	12.00	15.00	19.00
1812 2 over 1.................. }	1,628,059	12.00	14.00	20.00	40.00
1812 Normal date.............. }		11.00	13.00	16.00	20.00
1813	1,241,903	11.00	13.00	16.00	20.00
1814 4 over 3.................. }	1,039,075	11.00	14.00	20.00	35.00
1814 Normal date.............. }		10.00	12.00	15.00	19.00
1815 5 over 2..................	47,150	95.00	120.00	210.00	300.00
1817 7 over 3..................		15.00	19.00	25.00	40.00
1817 dated 181.7.............. }	1,215,567	15.00	19.00	25.00	40.00
1817 Normal date..............		10.00	12.00	15.00	19.00
1818 8 over 7.................. }	1,960,322	10.00	12.00	15.00	19.00
1818 Normal date.............. }		10.00	12.00	15.00	19.00
1819 9 over 8.................. }	2,208,000	10.00	13.00	16.00	20.00
1819 Normal date.............. }		10.00	13.00	16.00	20.00
1820 20 over 19................ }	751,122	11.00	14.00	17.50	22.00
1820 Normal date.............. }		11.00	14.00	17.50	22.00
1821	1,305,797	10.00	12.00	15.00	19.00
1822 2 over 1.................. }	1,559,573	20.00	30.00	40.00	60.00
1822 Normal date.............. }		10.00	12.00	15.00	19.00
1823	1,694,200	10.00	12.00	14.00	18.00
1824 4 over 1..................		10.00	12.00	15.00	19.00
1824 over other dates.......... }	3,504,954	10.00	12.00	15.00	19.00
1824 Normal date..............		10.00	12.00	14.00	18.00
1825	2,943,166	10.00	12.00	14.00	18.00
1826	4,004,180	10.00	12.00	14.00	18.00
1827 7 over 6.................. }	5,493,400	11.00	13.00	16.00	21.00
1827 Normal date.............. }		10.00	12.00	14.00	18.00
1828 .... }	3,075,200	10.00	12.00	14.00	18.00
1828 Curled-base, knobbed 2..... }		17.50	22.50	30.00	45.00
1829 9 over 7.................. }	3,712,156	10.00	12.00	15.00	19.00
1829 Normal date.............. }		10.00	12.00	14.00	18.00
1830	4,764,800	10.00	12.00	14.00	18.00
1831	5,873,660	10.00	12.00	14.00	18.00
1832	4,797,000	10.00	12.00	14.00	18.00
1833	5,206,000	10.00	12.00	14.00	18.00
1834	6,412,004	10.00	12.00	14.00	18.00
1835	5,352,006	10.00	12.00	14.00	18.00
1836 Lettered edge..............	6,545,000	10.00	12.00	14.00	18.00

HALF DOLLARS
Variety 2 — Reeded edge, reverse "50 CENTS" 1836-1837

GOOD—*LIBERTY discernible on headband.*

V. GOOD—*Minimum of 3 letters in LIBERTY must be clear.*

FINE—*LIBERTY complete.*

V. FINE—*LIBERTY is sharp. Shoulder clasp is clear.*

	Quan. Minted	Good	V. Good	Fine	V. Fine
1836 Reeded edge....................	1,200	$150.00	$200.00	$325.00	$500.00
1837	3,629,820	15.00	20.00	30.00	40.00

Variety 3 — Reeded edge, reverse "HALF DOL." 1838-1839

The 1838O half dollar was not mentioned in Director's report. (Rufus Tyler, coiner of New Orleans Mint, stated that only 20 were coined.)

First branch mint half dollar. This and following year mint mark appears on Obv. All other years prior to 1968 (except 1916-17) mintmark is on the reverse.

1838	3,546,000	12.50	17.50	27.50	37.50
1838O..........................	(20)				——
1839 Bust type.......... All kinds	3,334,560	12.50	17.50	27.50	37.50
1839O..........................	178,976	40.00	65.00	85.00	110.00

LIBERTY SEATED TYPE 1839-1891
Variety 1 — No motto above eagle 1839-1853

GOOD—*Scant rim. LIBERTY on shield worn off. Date and letters readable.*

V. GOOD—*Rim fairly defined. At least 3 letters in LIBERTY are evident.*

FINE—*LIBERTY complete, but weak.*

V. FINE—*LIBERTY mostly sharp.*

1839 Liberty seated, no drapery		17.50	22.50	35.00	65.00
1839 Liberty seated, drapery at elbow......		7.50	8.50	13.00	21.00
1840	1,435,008	6.50	7.50	12.00	18.00
1840O..........................	855,100	6.50	7.50	12.00	18.00
1841	310,000	8.50	10.00	15.00	23.00
1841O...:..........................	401,000	6.50	7.50	12.00	18.00

HALF DOLLARS

	Quan. Minted	Good	V. Good	Fine	V. Fine
1842	2,012,764	$6.50	$7.50	$12.00	$18.00
1842O Small date	} 957,000	45.00	85.00	135.00	200.00
1842O Larger date		6.50	7.50	12.00	18.00
1843	3,844,000	6.50	7.50	12.00	18.00
1843O	2,268,000	6.50	7.50	12.00	18.00
1844	1,766,000	6.50	7.50	12.00	18.00
1844O	2,005,000	6.50	7.50	12.00	18.00
1845	589,000	6.50	7.50	12.00	18.00
1845O	} 2,094,000	6.50	7.50	12.00	18.00
1845O No drapery		6.50	7.50	12.00	18.00
1846 Over horizontal 6 (error)	} 2,210,000	12.00	24.00	30.00	45.00
Normal date		6.50	7.50	12.00	18.00
1846O	2,304,000	6.50	7.50	12.00	18.00
1847 7 over 6	} 1,156,000	—	—	—	—
1847 Normal date		6.50	7.50	12.00	18.00
1847O	2,584,000	6.50	7.50	12.00	18.00
1848	580,000	9.00	14.00	20.00	30.00
1848O	3,180,000	6.50	7.50	12.00	18.00
1849	1,252,000	6.50	7.50	12.00	18.00
1849O	2,310,000	6.50	7.50	12.00	18.00
1850	227,000	15.00	21.00	35.00	45.00
1850O	2,456,000	6.50	7.50	12.00	18.00
1851	200,750	15.00	21.00	35.00	45.00
1851O	402,000	6.50	7.50	12.00	18.00
1852	77,130	22.50	35.00	50.00	110.00
1852O	144,000	15.00	21.00	35.00	45.00
1853O No arrows or rays. (Ex. rare)					
Beware of 1858-O altered date		—	—	—	—

**Variety 2 —
Arrows at date,
rays around eagle
1853 only**

1853	3,532,708	8.00	11.00	17.00	45.00
1853O	1,328,000	8.00	11.00	17.00	45.00

Variety 3 — Arrows at date, no rays 1854-1855

1854	2,982,000	7.00	8.50	12.50	19.00
1854O	5,240,000	7.00	8.50	12.50	19.00
1855	759,500	7.00	8.50	12.50	19.00
1855O	3,688,000	7.00	8.50	12.50	19.00
1855S	129,950	30.00	60.00	90.00	175.00

Variety 1 design resumed 1856-1866

1856	938,000	6.00	7.00	11.00	16.00
1856O	2,658,000	6.00	7.00	11.00	16.00
1856S	211,000	8.00	9.50	16.00	42.00
1857	1,988,000	6.00	7.00	11.00	16.00

HALF DOLLARS

	Quan. Minted	Good	V. Good	Fine	V. Fine
1857O	818,000	$6.00	$7.00	$11.00	$16.00
1857S	158,000	9.00	13.00	21.00	42.50
1858	4,226,000	6.00	7.00	11.00	16.00
1858O	7,294,000	6.00	7.00	11.00	16.00
1858S	476,000	7.00	9.00	13.00	20.00
1859	748,000	6.00	7.00	11.00	16.00
1859O	2,834,000	6.00	7.00	11.00	16.00
1859S	566,000	6.00	7.00	11.00	16.00
1860	303,700	6.00	7.00	11.00	16.00
1860O	1,290,000	6.00	7.00	11.00	16.00
1860S	472,000	7.00	9.00	13.00	20.00
1861	2,888,400	6.00	7.00	11.00	16.00
1861O*	2,532,633	6.00	7.00	11.00	16.00
1861 Confederate reverse (restrike)					250.00
1861S	939,500	6.00	7.00	11.00	16.00
1862	253,550	8.00	10.00	15.00	22.50
1862S	1,352,000	6.00	7.00	11.00	16.00
1863	503,660	6.00	7.00	11.00	16.00
1863S	916,000	6.00	7.00	11.00	16.00
1864	379,570	6.00	7.00	11.00	16.00
1864S	658,000	6.00	7.00	11.00	16.00
1865	511,900	6.00	7.00	11.00	16.00
1865S	675,000	6.00	7.00	11.00	16.00
1866S No motto. All kinds	1,054,000	22.50	37.50	60.00	120.00

*The 1861O quantity includes 330,000 struck under the United States government; 1,240,000 for the State of Louisiana after it seceded from the Union; and 962,633 after Louisiana joined the Confederate States of America. As all these 1861O coins were struck from U.S. dies it is impossible to distinguish one from another. They should not be confused with the very rare Confederate half dollar of 1861, which has a distinctive reverse.

Variety 4 —
Motto "In God We Trust"
added above eagle 1866-1873

	Quan. Minted	Good	V. Good	Fine	V. Fine
1866	745,625	6.00	7.00	11.00	16.00
1866S With motto		6.00	7.00	11.00	16.00
1867	449,925	6.00	7.00	11.00	16.00
1867S	1,196,000	6.00	7.00	11.00	16.00
1868	418,200	6.00	7.00	11.00	16.00
1868S	1,160,000	6.00	7.00	11.00	16.00
1869	795,900	6.00	7.00	11.00	16.00
1869S	656,000	6.00	7.00	11.00	16.00
1870	634,900	6.00	7.00	11.00	16.00
1870CC	54,617	60.00	110.00	225.00	325.00
1870S	1,004,000	6.00	7.00	11.00	16.00
1871	1,204,560	6.00	7.00	11.00	16.00
1871CC	153,950	24.00	35.00	65.00	110.00
1871S	2,178,000	6.00	7.00	11.00	16.00

HALF DOLLARS

	Quan. Minted	Good	V. Good	Fine	V. Fine
1872	881,550	$6.00	$7.00	$11.00	$16.00
1872CC	257,000	15.00	22.50	37.50	75.00
1872S	580,000	6.00	7.00	11.00	16.00
1873 No arrows	801,800	6.00	7.00	11.00	16.00
1873CC No arrows	122,500	21.00	35.00	65.00	125.00
1873S No arrows	5,000	Unknown in any collection.			

Variety 5 — Arrows at date 1873-1874

1873 Arrows at date	1,815,700	9.50	15.00	22.00	45.00
1873CC Arrows	214,560	15.00	24.00	50.00	85.00
1873S Arrows	228,000	13.50	22.00	30.00	55.00
1874 Arrows	2,360,300	9.50	15.00	22.00	45.00
1874CC Arrows	59,000	20.00	35.00	80.00	125.00
1874S Arrows	394,000	15.00	23.00	35.00	70.00

Variety 4 resumed 1875-1891

1875	6,027,500	6.00	7.00	11.00	16.00
1875CC	1,008,000	6.50	8.50	12.50	20.00
1875S	3,200,000	6.00	7.00	11.00	16.00
1876	8,419,150	6.00	7.00	11.00	16.00
1876CC	1,956,000	6.00	7.00	11.00	16.00
1876S	4,528,000	6.00	7.00	11.00	16.00
1877	8,304,510	6.00	7.00	11.00	16.00
1877CC	1,420,000	7.00	8.00	12.00	18.00
1877S	5,356,000	6.00	7.00	11.00	16.00
1878	1,378,400	6.00	7.00	11.00	16.00
1878CC	62,000	55.00	75.00	125.00	190.00
1878S	12,000	600.00	900.00	1,400	2,000
1879	5,900	50.00	60.00	70.00	90.00
1880	9,755	45.00	55.00	65.00	85.00
1881	10,975	42.50	52.50	62.50	80.00
1882	5,500	50.00	60.00	70.00	90.00
1883	9,039	45.00	55.00	65.00	85.00
1884	5,275	50.00	60.00	70.00	90.00
1885	6,130	50.00	60.00	70.00	90.00
1886	5,886	55.00	65.00	75.00	100.00
1887	5,710	50.00	60.00	70.00	90.00
1888	12,833	35.00	45.00	50.00	65.00
1889	12,711	35.00	45.00	50.00	65.00
1890	12,590	35.00	45.00	50.00	65.00
1891	200,600	6.00	7.00	11.00	16.00

BARBER or LIBERTY HEAD TYPE 1892-1915

Like the dime and quarter of this period, the half dollar was designed by Charles E. Barber. His initial B is at the truncation of the neck.

GOOD—*Date and legends readable. LIBERTY worn off headband.*

FINE—*LIBERTY completely readable, but not sharp.*

V. FINE—*All letters in LIBERTY evenly plain.*

HALF DOLLARS

Quan. Minted	Gd.	Fine	V.F.	Quan. Minted	Gd.	Fine	V.F.
1892...... 935,245	$4.50	$15.00	$25.00	1904O.... 1,117,600	$3.00	$8.00	$24.00
1892O..... 390,000	50.00	90.00	125.00	1904S..... 553,038	6.00	19.00	45.00
1892S.... 1,029,028	40.00	60.00	90.00	1905...... 662,727	3.25	12.00	25.00
1893..... 1,826,792	4.50	15.00	25.00	1905O..... 505,000	5.00	16.00	37.50
1893O.... 1,389,000	10.00	22.00	45.00	1905S.... 2,494,000	3.00	8.00	23.00
1893S..... 740,000	31.00	57.00	90.00	1906..... 2,638,675	3.00	8.00	23.00
1894..... 1,148,972	4.50	15.00	25.00	1906D ... 4,028,000	3.00	8.00	23.00
1894O.... 2,138,000	4.50	15.00	25.00	1906O.... 2,446,000	3.00	8.00	23.00
1894S.... 4,048,690	3.50	13.00	24.00	1906S.... 1,740,154	3.00	8.00	23.00
1895..... 1,835,218	3.50	13.00	24.00	1907..... 2,598,575	3.00	8.00	23.00
1895O.... 1,766,000	4.50	15.00	25.00	1907D ... 3,856,000	3.00	8.00	23.00
1895S.... 1,108,086	9.50	20.00	38.00	1907O.... 3,946,600	3.00	8.00	23.00
1896...... 950,762	4.50	15.00	25.00	1907S.... 1,250,000	3.00	8.00	23.00
1896O..... 924,000	7.50	20.00	50.00	1908..... 1,354,545	3.00	8.00	23.00
1896S.... 1,140,948	30.00	50.00	70.00	1908D ... 3,280,000	3.00	8.00	23.00
1897..... 2,480,731	3.00	10.00	23.00	1908O.... 5,360,000	3.00	8.00	23.00
1897O.... 632,000	20.00	45.00	75.00	1908S.... 1,644,828	3.00	8.00	23.00
1897S..... 933,900	24.00	47.50	80.00	1909..... 2,368,650	3.00	8.00	23.00
1898..... 2,956,735	3.00	8.00	23.00	1909O..... 925,400	3.00	8.00	23.00
1898O.... 874,000	5.00	16.00	30.00	1909S.... 1,764,000	3.00	8.00	23.00
1898S.... 2,358,550	3.50	9.00	24.00	1910...... 418,551	3.50	12.00	26.00
1899..... 5,538,846	3.00	8.00	23.00	1910S.... 1,948,000	3.00	8.00	23.00
1899O.... 1,724,000	3.00	8.00	24.00	1911..... 1,406,543	3.00	8.00	23.00
1899S.... 1,686,411	4.25	12.00	24.00	1911D 695,080	3.00	8.00	23.00
1900..... 4,762,912	3.00	8.00	23.00	1911S.... 1,272,000	3.00	8.00	23.00
1900O.... 2,744,000	3.00	8.00	23.00	1912..... 1,550,700	3.00	8.00	23.00
1900S.... 2,560,322	3.00	8.00	23.00	1912D ... 2,300,800	3.00	8.00	23.00
1901..... 4,268,813	3.00	8.00	23.00	1912S.... 1,370,000	3.00	8.00	23.00
1901O.... 1,124,000	3.00	12.00	38.00	1913...... 188,627	8.00	17.50	45.00
1901S..... 847,044	5.50	30.00	75.00	1913D 534,000	3.00	8.00	24.00
1902..... 4,922,777	3.00	8.00	23.00	1913S..... 604,000	3.00	8.00	24.00
1902O.... 2,526,000	3.00	8.00	23.00	1914...... 124,610	12.00	30.00	62.50
1902S.... 1,460,670	3.00	8.00	23.00	1914S..... 992,000	3.00	8.00	23.00
1903..... 2,278,755	3.00	8.00	23.00	1915...... 138,450	10.00	22.00	45.00
1903O.... 2,100,000	3.00	8.00	23.00	1915D ... 1,170,400	3.00	8.00	23.00
1903S.... 1,920,772	3.00	8.00	24.00	1915S.... 1,604,000	3.00	8.00	23.00
1904..... 2,992,670	3.00	8.00	23.00				

LIBERTY WALKING TYPE 1916-1947

The designer of this attractive coin was A. A. Weinman, whose monogram AW appears under the tip of the wing feathers.

GOOD—Most of IN GOD WE TRUST is visible.

V. GOOD—Motto is distinct. About half of skirt lines at left are clear.

FINE—All skirt lines evident, but worn in spots. Details in sandal below motto are clear.

V. FINE—Lines on skirt incomplete. Lines in sandal complete but not bold. Some wear on breast and arm.

HALF DOLLARS

Proof totals shown in parentheses.

	Quan. Minted	Good	V. Good	Fine	V. Fine
1916	608,000	$6.00	$9.00	$15.00	$25.00
1916D on obv.	1,014,400	3.25	5.50	9.00	19.00
1916S on obv.	508,000	14.00	19.00	42.00	70.00
1917	12,292,000	3.00	3.00	3.50	4.00
1917D on obv.	765,400	3.25	4.75	10.00	24.00
1917D on rev.	1,940,000	3.25	3.50	4.50	15.00
1917S on obv.	952,000	3.50	6.00	16.00	40.00
1917S on rev.	5,554,000	3.00	3.00	3.50	7.00
1918	6,634,000	3.00	3.00	3.50	8.00
1918D	3,853,040	3.00	3.00	4.00	14.00
1918S	10,282,000	3.00	3.00	3.25	6.50
1919	962,000	3.25	3.75	9.00	30.00
1919D	1,165,000	3.00	3.50	8.00	37.50
1919S	1,552,000	3.00	3.50	7.50	35.00
1920	6,372,000	3.00	3.00	3.00	6.00
1920D	1,551,000	3.00	3.00	5.00	25.00
1920S	4,624,000	3.00	3.00	3.50	14.00
1921	246,000	24.00	32.00	55.00	125.00
1921D	208,000	40.00	50.00	85.00	145.00
1921S	548,000	4.50	8.00	15.00	65.00
1923S	2,178,000	3.00	3.00	3.00	17.00
1927S	2,392,000	3.00	3.00	3.00	6.00
1928S	1,940,000	3.00	3.00	3.00	5.50
1929D	1,001,200	3.00	3.00	3.00	5.00
1929S	1,902,000			3.00	3.50
1933S	1,786,000			3.00	3.25
1934	6,964,000			3.00	3.00
1934D	2,361,400			3.00	3.00
1934S	3,652,000			3.00	3.00
1935	9,162,000			3.00	3.00
1935D	3,003,800			3.00	3.00
1935S	3,854,000			3.00	3.00
1936 (3,901)	12,617,901			3.00	3.00
1936D	4,252,400			3.00	3.00
1936S	3,884,000			3.00	3.00
1937 (5,728)	9,527,728			3.00	3.00
1937D	1,676,000		3.00	3.00	4.00
1937S	2,090,000			3.00	3.00
1938 (8,152)	4,118,152			3.00	3.00
1938D	491,600	14.00	15.00	18.00	25.00
1939 (8,808)	6,820,808			3.00	3.00
1939D	4,267,800			3.00	3.00
1939S	2,552,000			3.00	3.00
1940 (11,279)	9,167,279			3.00	3.00
1940S	4,550,000			3.00	3.00
1941 (15,412)	24,207,412			3.00	3.00
1941D	11,248,400			3.00	3.00
1941S	8,098,000			3.00	3.50
1942 (21,120)	47,839,120			3.00	3.00
1942D	10,973,800			3.00	3.00
1942S	12,708,000			3.00	3.00
1943	53,190,000			3.00	3.00
1943D	11,346,000			3.00	3.00

HALF DOLLARS

	Quan. Minted	Fine	V. Fine
1943S	13,450,000		$3.00
1944	28,206,000		3.00
1944D	9,769,000		3.00
1944S	8,904,000		3.00
1945	31,502,000		3.00
1945D	9,966,800		3.00
1945S	10,156,000		3.00
1946	12,118,000		3.00
1946D	2,151,000	$3.00	3.50
1946S	3,724,000		3.00
1947	4,094,000		3.00
1947D	3,900,600		3.00

FRANKLIN TYPE 1948-1963

John R. Sinnock was the designer of this type. His initials JRS appear under the shoulder.

FINE—*Designer's initials JRS distinct and clearly separated.*

V. FINE—*Half of incused lines on bell must show.*

EX. FINE—*Wear spots appear at top of end curls and hair back of ears. On reverse, Liberty bell will show wear at top.*

	Quan. Minted	Fine	V.F.	Ex. F.
1948	3,006,814	$3.00	$3.50	$3.75
1948D	4,028,600	2.75	2.75	3.00
1949	5,614,000	2.75	2.75	3.50
1949D	4,120,600	2.75	2.75	3.50
1949S	3,744,000	2.75	2.75	3.50
1950 (51,386)	7,793,509	2.75	2.75	2.75
1950D	8,031,600		2.75	2.75
1951 (57,500)	16,859,602		2.75	2.75
1951D	9,475,200		2.75	2.75
1951S	13,696,000		2.75	2.75
1952 (81,980)	21,274,073		2.75	2.75
1952D	25,395,600		2.75	2.75
1952S	5,526,000		2.75	2.75
1953 (128,800)	2,796,920	2.75	3.00	3.50
1953D	20,900,400			2.75
1953S	4,148,000			2.75
1954 (233,300)	13,421,503			2.75
1954D	25,445,580			2.75
1954S	4,993,400			2.75
1955 (378,200)	2,876,381	4.00	4.25	4.75
1956 (669,384)	4,701,384			2.75
1957 (1,247,952)	6,361,952			2.75
1957D	19,966,850			2.75
1958 (875,652)	4,917,652			2.75
1958D	23,962,412			2.75
1959 (1,149,291)	7,349,291			2.75
1959D	13,053,750			2.75

Common silver coins vary in value according to the prevailing price of silver.

[72]

HALF DOLLARS

	Quan. Minted	Ex. F.		Quan. Minted	Ex. F.
1960 (1,691,602)	7,715,602	$2.75	1962 (3,218,019)	12,932,019	$2.75
1960D	18,215,812	2.75	1962D	35,473,281	2.75
1961 (3,028,244)	11,318,244	2.75	1963 (3,075,645)	25,239,645	2.75
1961D	20,276,442	2.75	1963D	67,069,292	2.75

KENNEDY TYPE 1964 to Date

Gilroy Roberts, former Chief Engraver of the Mint, designed the obverse of this coin. His stylized initials are on the truncation of the forceful bust of President John F. Kennedy. The reverse, which uses the Presidential Coat of Arms for the motif, is the work of Frank Gasparro.

SILVER

		Ex. F.
1964 (3,950,762)	277,254,766	2.75
1964D	156,205,446	2.75

SILVER CLAD

1965	65,879,366	1.00
1966	108,984,932	1.00
1967	295,046,978	1.00
1968D	246,951,930	1.00
1968S Proof only	(3,041,506)	1.50
1969D	129,881,800	1.00
1969S Proof only	(2,934,631)	1.50
1970D	2,150,000	12.00
1970S Proof only	(2,632,810)	3.50

COPPER-NICKEL CLAD

1971	155,164,000	.50
1971D	302,097,424	.50
1971S Proof only	(3,220,733)	1.50

		Ex. F.
1972	153,180,000	.50
1972D	141,890,000	.50
1972S Proof only	(3,260,996)	1.50
1973	64,964,000	.50
1973D	83,171,400	.50
1973S Proof only	(2,760,339)	2.00
1974	201,596,000	.50
1974D	79,066,300	.50
1974S Proof only	(2,612,568)	2.00
1977	43,598,000	.50
1977D	31,449,106	.50
1977S Proof only	(3,251,152)	1.50
1978	14,350,000	.50
1978D	13,765,799	.50
1978S Proof only	(3,127,781)	2.00
1979		.50
1979D		.50
1979S Proof only		1.50

BICENTENNIAL COINAGE DATED 1776-1976

In October 1973 the Treasury announced an open contest for the selection of suitable designs for the special Bicentennial reverses of the quarter, half dollar, and dollar. Seth G. Huntington's winning entry is featured on the half dollar. It shows Independence Hall in Philadelphia as the center device. The obverse is unchanged except for the dual dating 1776-1976. These dual-dated pieces were struck during 1975 and 1976 for general circulation as well as for inclusion in special proof and mint sets.

HALF DOLLARS

	Quan. Minted	Unc.	Proof
1976 Copper-nickel clad	234,308,000	$ .50	
1976D Copper-nickel clad	287,565,248	.50	
1976S Copper-nickel clad (Proof only)	(7,059,099)		$1.00
1976S Silver clad	4,239,722	1.50	2.00

SILVER DOLLARS

Major types of silver dollars are few, although the early dates are plentiful in die varieties. The first date, 1794, is quite rare. The bust type was adopted in the latter part of 1795 and all dates of this type are fairly common except one — the famous 1804. The 1804 silver dollar has been the most discussed coin in American numismatics. There are those that are called "originals" of which eight specimens are known, and those called "restrikes" of which seven specimens are known. Fake 1804's have been made by altering 1801's which are of the same general type; some of these altered dates are very cleverly done and almost defy detection.

Silver dollars of 1836, 1838 and 1839 are patterns. About 1,000 pieces of the common type 1836 were struck; of the other varieties only a very limited number were struck.

After 1840 all silver dollars are relatively available with exception of just a few dates, 1851, 1852, 1858, etc.

FLOWING HAIR TYPE 1794-1795

FAIR—*Clear enough to identify.*
GOOD—*Date and letters readable. Main devices outlined, but lack details.*
V. GOOD—*Major details discernible. Letters well formed but worn.*
FINE—*Hair ends distinguishable. Top hairlines show, but otherwise worn smooth.*
V. FINE—*Hair in center shows some detail. Other details more bold.*

	Quan. Minted	Fair	Good	V. Good	Fine	V. Fine
1794	1,758	$1,000	$2,000	$3,000	$4,500	$7,500
1795 All kinds	203,033	135.00	225.00	300.00	400.00	550.00

DRAPED BUST TYPE, SMALL EAGLE REVERSE 1795-1798

FAIR—*Clear enough to identify.*
GOOD—*Bust outlined, no detail. Date readable, some leaves evident.*
V. GOOD—*Drapery worn except deepest folds. Hairlines smooth.*
FINE—*All drapery lines distinguishable. Hairlines near cheek and neck show some detail.*
V. FINE—*Left side of drapery worn smooth.*

[74]

SILVER DOLLARS

	Quan. Minted	Fair	Good	V. Good	Fine	V. Fine
1795 Bust type		$120.00	$200.00	$225.00	$325.00	$475.00
1796	72,920	100.00	165.00	210.00	300.00	425.00
1797	7,776	100.00	165.00	210.00	300.00	425.00
1798 All kinds	327,536	100.00	155.00	200.00	285.00	400.00

DRAPED BUST TYPE, HERALDIC EAGLE REVERSE 1798-1804

GOOD—*Letters and date are readable. E. PLURIBUS UNUM obliterated.*
V. GOOD—*Motto partially readable. Only deepest drapery details visible. All other lines smooth.*
FINE—*All drapery lines distinguishable. Hairlines near cheek and neck show some detail.*
V. FINE—*Left side of drapery is worn smooth.*

	Quan. Minted	Good	V. Good	Fine	V. Fine
1798 Heraldic eagle		$140.00	$165.00	$270.00	$335.00
1799	423,515	140.00	165.00	270.00	335.00
1800	220,920	140.00	165.00	270.00	335.00
1801	54,454	140.00	165.00	270.00	335.00
1802	41,650	140.00	165.00	270.00	335.00
1803	85,634	140.00	165.00	270.00	335.00
1804 Variety 1, letter O in "OF" above cloud					Proof $120,000
Variety 2, letter O above space between clouds					Proof $100,000

GOBRECHT SILVER DOLLARS

Silver dollars of 1836, 1838 and 1839 were mostly made as trial pieces but some were made in quantities for general circulation. There was no regular issue of dollars 1805 to 1835 inclusive. The figures given for the following three years are approximate, as restrikes of many varieties are known to have been made. There are several other patterns of the 1836-1839 series, all extremely rare and seldom available.

SILVER DOLLARS

	Quan. Minted	V. Fine	Proof
1836 Obv. with name on base.			
Rev. with stars. Plain edge 1,000		$1,000	$2,400
1838 Obv. without name, stars added around border.			
Rev. with stars. Reeded edge 25			3,500
1839 Rev. without stars. Reeded edge 300		1,200	3,000

LIBERTY SEATED TYPE — Regular Issues 1840-1873
Variety 1 — No motto above eagle 1840-1865

V. GOOD—*Any three letters of LIBERTY should be at least two-thirds complete.*
FINE—*All drapery lines show but partly worn. Hair from brow, over ear and down neck, well outlined but shows only slight detail.*
V. FINE—*LIBERTY is strong and its ribbon shows slight wear.*

	Quan. Minted	V. Good	Fine	V. Fine
1840 61,005		$55.00	$65.00	$85.00
1841 173,000		50.00	60.00	75.00
1842 184,618		50.00	60.00	75.00
1843 165,100		50.00	60.00	75.00
1844 20,000		65.00	75.00	100.00
1845 24,500		65.00	75.00	100.00
1846 110,600		50.00	60.00	80.00
1846O 59,000		65.00	75.00	100.00
1847 140,750		50.00	60.00	80.00
1848 15,000		60.00	70.00	95.00
1849 62,600		50.00	65.00	85.00

SILVER DOLLARS

	Quan. Minted	V. Good	Fine	V. Fine
1850	7,500	$65.00	$75.00	$120.00
1850O	40,000	55.00	65.00	85.00
1851 (Original)	1,300			900.00
1852 (Original)	1,100			*Unc.* 2,800
1853	46,110	55.00	65.00	90.00
1854	33,140	65.00	75.00	120.00
1855	26,000	65.00	75.00	120.00
1856	63,500	60.00	70.00	90.00
1857	94,000	57.50	65.00	80.00
1858 (Not in Mint Director's report)	Est. 80			*Proof* 2,100
1859	256,500	50.00	60.00	75.00
1859O	360,000	50.00	60.00	75.00
1859S	20,000	57.50	75.00	90.00
1860	218,930	50.00	60.00	75.00
1860O	515,000	50.00	60.00	75.00
1861	78,500	52.50	62.50	80.00
1862	12,090	60.00	70.00	85.00
1863	27,660	50.00	65.00	85.00
1864	31,170	50.00	65.00	85.00
1865	47,000	50.00	65.00	85.00

Variety 2 —
Motto "In God We Trust"
added above eagle 1866-1873

	Quan. Minted	V. Good	Fine	V. Fine
1866 With motto	49,625	55.00	65.00	80.00
1867	47,525	55.00	65.00	80.00
1868	162,700	50.00	60.00	75.00
1869	424,300	50.00	60.00	75.00
1870	416,000	50.00	60.00	75.00
1870CC	12,462	65.00	80.00	120.00
1870S	—			—
1871	1,074,760	50.00	60.00	75.00
1871CC	1,376	325.00	450.00	675.00
1872	1,106,450	50.00	60.00	75.00
1872CC	3,150	175.00	225.00	350.00
1872S	9,000	65.00	75.00	120.00
1873	293,600	50.00	60.00	75.00
1873CC	2,300	375.00	600.00	950.00
1873S	700	Unknown in any collection		

LIBERTY HEAD or MORGAN TYPE 1878-1921

SILVER DOLLARS
LIBERTY HEAD or MORGAN TYPE 1878-1921

George T. Morgan designed the silver dollar which was first issued in 1878. This type is sometimes known as the "Bland" dollar, after Richard P. Bland, co-author of the Bland Silver Bill of 1878 which provided for the new design.

270,232,722 silver dollars were melted under the Pittman Act of April, 1918, which probably accounts for the scarcity of some dates.

V. FINE—*Two-thirds of hairlines from top of forehead to ear must show. Ear well defined. Feathers on eagle's breast worn at center.*

EX. FINE—*All hairlines strong and ear bold. Eagle's feathers all plain but slight wear on breast and wing tips.*

	Quan. Minted	V. Fine	Ex. Fine	Unc.
1878 8 tail feathers	⎫ 10,509,550	$8.00	$9.50	$30.00
1878 7 tail feathers	⎭	8.00	9.00	25.00
1878CC	2,212,000	10.00	13.00	50.00
1878S	9,774,000	7.50	8.50	18.00
1879	14,807,100	7.50	8.50	18.50
1879CC	756,000	35.00	90.00	500.00
1879O	2,887,000	7.50	8.50	37.50
1879S	9,110,000	7.50	8.50	15.00
1880	12,601,355	7.50	8.50	18.00
1880CC	591,000	25.00	33.00	85.00
1880O	5,305,000	7.50	9.00	35.00
1880S	8,900,000	7.50	8.50	13.00
1881	9,163,975	7.50	8.50	16.00
1881CC	296,000	40.00	47.50	90.00
1881O	5,708,000	7.50	8.50	13.00
1881S	12,760,000	7.50	8.50	13.00
1882	11,101,000	7.50	8.50	15.00
1882CC	1,133,000	10.00	14.00	32.50
1882O	6,090,000	7.50	8.50	13.00
1882S	9,250,000	7.50	8.50	13.00
1883	12,291,039	7.50	8.50	15.00
1883CC	1,204,000	11.00	14.00	31.00
1883O	8,725,000	7.50	8.50	12.00
1883S	6,250,000	8.00	9.00	250.00
1884	14,070,875	7.50	8.50	27.50
1884CC	1,136,000	14.00	17.00	32.00
1884O	9,730,000	7.50	8.50	12.00
1884S	3,200,000	8.00	12.50	625.00
1885	17,787,767	7.50	8.50	12.00
1885CC	228,000	60.00	70.00	100.00
1885O	9,185,000	7.50	8.50	12.00
1885S	1,497,000	8.00	10.00	70.00
1886	19,963,886	7.50	8.50	12.00
1886O	10,710,000	7.50	9.00	190.00
1886S	750,000	12.00	17.00	140.00
1887	20,290,710	7.50	8.50	12.00
1887O	11,550,000	7.50	8.50	32.50
1887S	1,771,000	7.50	9.00	60.00
1888	19,183,833	7.50	8.50	13.00
1888O	12,150,000	7.50	8.50	22.50
1888S	657,000	15.00	20.00	135.00
1889	21,726,811	7.50	8.50	12.00
1889CC	350,000	140.00	290.00	3,100
1889O	11,875,000	7.50	8.50	80.00

SILVER DOLLARS

	Quan. Minted	V. Fine	Ex. Fine	Unc.
1889S	700,000	$14.00	$17.50	$125.00
1890	16,802,590	7.50	8.50	23.00
1890CC	2,309,041	11.00	17.50	95.00
1890O	10,701,000	7.50	8.50	37.50
1890S	8,230,373	7.50	8.50	35.00
1891	8,694,206	7.50	8.50	100.00
1891CC	1,618,000	11.00	17.50	85.00
1891O	7,954,529	7.50	9.00	85.00
1891S	5,296,000	7.50	8.50	35.00
1892	1,037,245	7.50	9.00	75.00
1892CC	1,352,000	22.00	50.00	250.00
1892O	2,744,000	7.50	8.50	90.00
1892S	1,200,000	15.00	75.00	3,750
1893	378,792	22.50	40.00	225.00
1893CC	677,000	50.00	160.00	525.00
1893O	300,000	40.00	75.00	600.00
1893S	100,000	650.00	1,500	——
1894	110,972	175.00	250.00	625.00
1894O	1,723,000	9.00	13.00	400.00
1894S	1,260,000	13.50	35.00	215.00
1895 (Beware removed mint mark)	12,880		*Proof*	$7,500
1895O	450,000	50.00	90.00	1,200
1895S	400,000	80.00	210.00	875.00
1896	9,976,762	7.50	8.50	14.50
1896O	4,900,000	8.00	9.50	250.00
1896S	5,000,000	12.00	36.00	400.00
1897	2,822,731	7.50	8.50	20.00
1897O	4,004,000	7.50	9.00	200.00
1897S	5,825,000	7.50	8.50	39.00
1898	5,884,735	7.50	8.50	17.00
1898O	4,440,000	7.50	8.50	13.00
1898S	4,102,000	8.00	10.00	185.00
1899	330,846	15.00	23.50	60.00
1899O	12,290,000	7.50	8.50	13.00
1899S	2,562,000	8.50	13.00	200.00
1900	8,830,912	7.50	8.50	13.50
1900O	12,590,000	7.50	8.50	13.00
1900S	3,540,000	8.00	10.00	75.00
1901	6,962,813	10.00	23.00	575.00
1901O	13,320,000	7.50	8.50	18.00
1901S	2,284,000	9.50	15.00	110.00
1902	7,994,777	7.50	8.50	45.00
1902O	8,636,000	7.50	8.50	12.00
1902S	1,530,000	25.00	39.00	140.00
1903	4,652,755	7.50	8.50	40.00
1903O	4,450,000	40.00	50.00	115.00
1903S	1,241,000	12.00	60.00	900.00
1904	2,788,650	8.00	9.00	85.00
1904O	3,720,000	7.50	8.50	12.00
1904S	2,304,000	10.00	40.00	500.00
1921	44,690,000	7.50	8.50	10.00
1921D	20,345,000	7.50	8.50	22.00
1921S	21,695,000	7.50	8.50	40.00

SILVER DOLLARS
PEACE TYPE 1921-1935

Agitation for a coin to commemorate the coming of peace after World War I started during the 1920 American Numismatic Association convention. Anthony de Francisci designed the new dollar, which was placed in circulation as a regular issue on January 3, 1922.

V. FINE—*Hair over eye well worn. Some strands over ear well defined. Some eagle feathers on top and outside edge of right wing will show.*

EX. FINE—*Hairlines over brow and ear are strong though slightly worn. Outside wing feathers at right and those at top are visible but faint.*

	Quan. Minted	V. Fine	Ex. Fine	Unc.
1921 Peace type	1,006,473	$18.00	$23.00	$125.00
1922	51,737,000	7.50	8.50	10.00
1922D	15,063,000	7.50	8.50	16.00
1922S	17,475,000	7.50	8.50	20.00
1923	30,800,000	7.50	8.50	10.00
1923D	6,811,000	7.50	8.50	25.00
1923S	19,020,000	7.50	8.50	26.50
1924	11,811,000	7.50	8.50	12.00
1924S	1,728,000	8.50	10.00	85.00
1925	10,198,000	7.50	8.50	11.00
1925S	1,610,000	7.50	9.00	60.00
1926	1,939,000	7.50	8.50	19.00
1926D	2,348,700	7.50	8.50	75.00
1926S	6,980,000	7.50	8.50	22.00
1927	848,000	12.00	15.00	50.00
1927D	1,268,900	8.50	11.00	170.00
1927S	866,000	8.00	10.00	110.00
1928	360,649	85.00	110.00	175.00
1928S	1,632,000	8.00	9.00	75.00
1934	954,057	9.00	11.00	50.00
1934D	1,569,500	9.00	11.00	70.00
1934S	1,011,000	13.00	65.00	700.00
1935	1,576,000	8.00	9.00	40.00
1935S	1,964,000	8.00	10.00	90.00

EISENHOWER DOLLAR 1971 To Date

Intended to honor both the late President Dwight D. Eisenhower and the first landing of man on the moon, this design is the work of Chief Engraver Frank Gasparro, whose initials are on the truncation and below the eagle. The reverse is an adaptation of the official Apollo 11 insignia. Collectors' coins were struck in 40% silver composition and the circulation issue in clad copper-nickel. Mint mark location is above the date.

SILVER DOLLARS

	Quan. Minted	Unc.		Quan. Minted	Unc.
1971	47,799,000	$1.00	1973S Silver		
1971D	68,587,424	1.00	(1,013,646)	1,883,140	$5.00
1971S Silver			1974	27,366,000	1.00
(4,265,234)	6,868,530	3.25	1974D	45,517,000	1.00
1972	75,890,000	1.00	1974S Proof	(2,612,568)	4.00
1972D	92,548,511	1.00	1974S Silver		
1972S Silver			(1,306,579)	1,900,000	4.00
(1,811,631)	2,193,056	4.25	1977	12,596,000	1.00
1973	1,769,258	10.00	1977D	32,983,006	1.00
1973D	1,769,258	10.00	1977S Proof	(3,251,152)	2.50
1973S Proof	(2,760,339)	3.50	1978	25,702,000	1.00
			1978D	23,012,290	1.00
			1978S Proof	(3,127,781)	7.00

BICENTENNIAL COINAGE DATED 1776-1976

The Bicentennial of the United States was highlighted by the introduction of new reverse designs for the quarter, half dollar, and dollar. The Liberty Bell superimposed on the moon was chosen for the reverse of the dollar. This design is the work of Dennis R. Williams. The obverse remained as before except for the dual dating 1776-1976. Pieces with this dating were struck during 1975 and 1976, for general circulation as well as special proof and mint sets.

	Quan. Minted	Unc.	Proof
1976 Copper-nickel clad	117,337,000	$1.00	
1976D Copper-nickel clad	103,228,274	1.00	
1976S Copper-nickel clad (Proof only)	(7,059,099)		$2.00
1976S Silver clad	(3,295,714) 4,239,722	3.25	6.25

ANTHONY DOLLARS 1979 to Date

1979P Copper-nickel clad	1.00	
1979D Copper-nickel clad	1.00	
1979S Copper-nickel clad	1.00	2.00

TRADE DOLLARS

(Coined from 1873 to 1885)

This coin was issued for circulation in the Orient to compete with the Mexican peso. When first coined they were legal tender in United States to the extent of $5.00 but with the decline in price of silver bullion Congress repealed the legal tender provision in 1876 and authorized the Treasury to limit coinage to export demand. In 1887 a law was passed authorizing the Treasury to redeem all Trade dollars which were not mutilated. U.S. Trade dollars are no longer circulating in the Orient. Those struck in the last few years of coinage were undoubtedly all proofs to satisfy collectors' demands.

The Trade dollars of 1884 and 1885 were unknown to collectors generally until 1908. None is listed in the Director's report. The law authorizing Trade dollars was repealed in February, 1887.

FINE—*Mottoes and LIBERTY readable but worn.*
EX. FINE—*Mottoes and LIBERTY are sharp. Only slight wear on rims.*

	Quan. Minted	V. Good	Fine	Ex. Fine	Unc.	Proof
1873	397,500	$30.00	$35.00	$60.00	$275.00	
1873CC	124,500	35.00	40.00	65.00	375.00	
1873S	703,000	30.00	35.00	60.00	275.00	
1874	987,800	30.00	35.00	50.00	250.00	
1874CC	1,373,200	35.00	40.00	65.00	300.00	
1874S	2,549,000	30.00	35.00	50.00	250.00	
1875	218,900	35.00	40.00	65.00	350.00	
1875CC	1,573,700	35.00	40.00	65.00	325.00	
1875S	4,487,000	30.00	35.00	50.00	250.00	
1876	456,150	30.00	35.00	50.00	250.00	
1876CC	509,000	35.00	40.00	65.00	300.00	
1876S	5,227,000	30.00	35.00	50.00	250.00	
1877	3,039,710	30.00	35.00	50.00	250.00	
1877CC	534,000	35.00	40.00	65.00	375.00	
1877S	9,519,000	30.00	35.00	50.00	250.00	
1878	900					$900.00
1878CC	97,000	65.00	100.00	200.00	1,500	
1878S	4,162,000	30.00	35.00	50.00	250.00	
1879	1,541					800.00
1880	1,987					800.00
1881	960					800.00
1882	1,097					800.00
1883	979					800.00
1884	10					——
1885	5					——

GOLD DOLLARS

Coinage of the gold dollar was begun in 1849; those coined 1849 to 1854 are known as the Liberty head or small sized type. In 1854 the piece was made larger in diameter and thinner and the design was changed to a feather headdress on a female, popularly known as the Indian head type or large size gold dollar (1854 was coined in both types). In 1856 the type was changed slightly by enlarging the size of the head.

Values for gold given in this handbook are for coins in "very good" or better condition. Dealers do not usually purchase gold coins on a bullion basis, therefore there is no numismatic market for gold in less than V. Good condition.

LIBERTY HEAD TYPE, 1849-1854

V. GOOD—*Partial LIBERTY on headband will show.*
FINE—*Full LIBERTY on headband. All hairlines and beads worn smooth.*
EX. FINE—*Little wear on hair, knobs on coronet must be bold.*

	Quan. Minted	Fine	V. Fine	Ex. Fine
1849	688,567	$120.00	$150.00	$170.00
1849C	11,634	175.00	225.00	300.00
1849D	21,588	150.00	200.00	275.00
1849O	215,000	120.00	150.00	170.00
1850	481,953	120.00	150.00	170.00
1850C	6,966	210.00	250.00	335.00
1850D	8,382	175.00	225.00	300.00
1850O	14,000	120.00	150.00	170.00
1851	3,317,671	120.00	150.00	170.00
1851C	41,267	190.00	240.00	320.00
1851D	9,882	200.00	250.00	325.00
1851O	290,000	120.00	150.00	170.00
1852	2,045,351	120.00	150.00	170.00
1852C	9,434	175.00	225.00	285.00
1852D	6,360	175.00	225.00	300.00
1852O	140,000	120.00	150.00	170.00
1853	4,076,051	120.00	150.00	170.00
1853C	11,515	175.00	225.00	300.00
1853D	6,583	175.00	225.00	300.00
1853O	290,000	120.00	150.00	170.00
1854	736,709	120.00	150.00	170.00
1854D	2,935	350.00	400.00	550.00
1854S	14,632	135.00	175.00	250.00

INDIAN HEAD TYPE, Small head 1854-1856

V. GOOD—*Feathers and headdress considerably worn.*
FINE—*Tips of feather curls on headdress partially worn away.*
EX. FINE—*Slight wear on headdress feather curls.*

1854	902,736	175.00	200.00	275.00
1855	758,269	175.00	200.00	275.00
1855C	9,803	325.00	375.00	775.00
1855D	1,811	1,700	1,900	2,400
1855O	55,000	250.00	300.00	450.00
1856S	24,600	200.00	250.00	325.00

GOLD DOLLARS
INDIAN HEAD TYPE, Large head 1856-1889

V. GOOD—*At least 3 letters show in LIBERTY.*
FINE—*Full LIBERTY in headband. Beads partially worn. Curled feathers worn flat.*
EX. FINE—*Trace of wear above and right of eye and on curled feathers.*

	Quan. Minted	Fine	V. Fine	Ex. Fine
1856	1,762,936	$100.00	$125.00	$150.00
1856D	1,460	1,450	2,000	3,000
1857	774,789	100.00	125.00	150.00
1857C	13,280	175.00	250.00	375.00
1857D	3,533	340.00	450.00	600.00
1857S	10,000	140.00	160.00	200.00
1858	117,995	100.00	125.00	150.00
1858D	3,477	450.00	500.00	750.00
1858S	10,000	140.00	175.00	225.00
1859	168,244	100.00	125.00	150.00
1859C	5,235	175.00	250.00	375.00
1859D	4,952	285.00	375.00	500.00
1859S	15,000	140.00	160.00	200.00
1860	36,668	100.00	125.00	150.00
1860D	1,566	1,650	2,000	2,750
1860S	13,000	140.00	160.00	200.00
1861	527,499	100.00	125.00	150.00
1861D		3,300	4,250	5,500
1862	1,361,390	100.00	125.00	150.00
1863	6,250	200.00	300.00	400.00
1864	5,950	175.00	210.00	275.00
1865	3,725	190.00	300.00	400.00
1866	7,130	150.00	190.00	250.00
1867	5,250	150.00	190.00	250.00
1868	10,525	140.00	160.00	200.00
1869	5,925	150.00	190.00	250.00
1870	6,335	140.00	160.00	200.00
1870S	3,000	410.00	550.00	750.00
1871	3,930	150.00	190.00	250.00
1872	3,530	150.00	190.00	250.00
1873	125,125	100.00	125.00	150.00
1874	198,820	100.00	125.00	150.00
1875	420	1,300	2,000	3,000
1876	3,245	150.00	170.00	225.00
1877	3,920	150.00	170.00	225.00
1878	3,020	150.00	170.00	225.00
1879	3,030	150.00	170.00	225.00
1880	1,636	150.00	170.00	225.00
1881	7,707	120.00	140.00	170.00
1882	5,125	120.00	140.00	170.00
1883	11,007	120.00	140.00	170.00
1884	6,236	120.00	140.00	170.00
1885	12,261	120.00	140.00	170.00
1886	6,016	120.00	140.00	170.00
1887	8,543	120.00	140.00	170.00
1888	16,580	120.00	140.00	170.00
1889	30,729	120.00	140.00	170.00

QUARTER EAGLES ($2.50 Gold Pieces)

Coinage began in 1796 and the last year is dated 1929. Most of the dates prior to 1834 are rare, some excessively rare; after 1834 only scattered dates are considered rare. One of these, 1848, has the letters CAL. over the eagle in reference to California gold.

CAPPED BUST TO RIGHT 1796-1807

V. GOOD—*Liberty's hair smooth. Only partial motto E PLURI-BUS UNUM.*

FINE—*Hair worn smooth on high spots. E PLURIBUS UNUM weak but readable.*

EX. FINE—*Slight wear on high spots.*

	Quan. Minted	V. Good	Fine	Ex. Fine
1796 No stars on obverse	963	$2,000	$4,500	$8,000

1796 With stars on obverse	432	1,700	3,500	7,000
1797	427	1,000	2,100	4,000
1798	1,094	900.00	1,500	3,000
1802 2 over 1	3,035	500.00	1,000	2,000
1804	3,327	500.00	1,000	2,000
1805	1,781	500.00	1,000	2,000
1806 6 over 4	} 1,616	700.00	1,300	2,500
1806 6 over 5		700.00	1,500	3,000
1807	6,812	500.00	900.00	1,800

CAPPED BUST TO LEFT 1808-1834

V. GOOD—*Half of E PLURIBUS UNUM shows. Part of Liberty shows.*

FINE—*E PLURIBUS UNUM and LIBERTY on headband readable but weak.*

EX. FINE—*Motto and LIBERTY sharp. Liberty's hair only slightly worn.*

1808	2,710	2,000	3,500	7,500
1821 Reduced size	6,448	600.00	1,200	2,600
1824 4 over 1	2,600	600.00	1,200	2,600
1825	4,434	600.00	1,200	2,600
1826 6 over 5	760	750.00	1,600	4,000
1827	2,800	600.00	1,200	2,600
1829	3,403	500.00	1,000	2,300
1830	4,540	500.00	1,000	2,300
1831	4,520	500.00	1,000	2,300
1832	4,400	500.00	1,000	2,300
1833	4,160	500.00	1,000	2,300
1834 With motto above eagle	4,000	900.00	2,000	4,500

QUARTER EAGLES ($2.50 Gold Pieces)

V. GOOD—*Partial LIBERTY.*

FINE—*LIBERTY readable and complete. Curl under ear outlined but no detail.*

EX. FINE—*Slight wear on hair at top of head, below "L" in LIBERTY, top of coronet and on reverse, upper wings and neck of eagle.*

	Quan. Minted	Fine	V. Fine	Ex. Fine
1834 Without motto	112,234	$100.00	$150.00	$225.00
1835	131,402	100.00	150.00	225.00
1836	547,986	100.00	150.00	225.00
1837	45,080	100.00	160.00	250.00
1838	47,030	100.00	160.00	250.00
1838C	7,880	200.00	250.00	435.00
1839	27,021	100.00	160.00	250.00
1839C	18,140	200.00	250.00	435.00
1839D	13,674	200.00	250.00	425.00
1839O	17,781	125.00	200.00	300.00

CORONET HEAD TYPE 1840-1907

	Quan. Minted	Fine	V. Fine	Ex. Fine
1840	18,859	75.00	100.00	140.00
1840C	12,822	125.00	175.00	300.00
1840D	3,532	170.00	225.00	400.00
1840O	33,580	75.00	100.00	140.00
1841 (Proofs only) Beware removed mint mark			*Proof*——	
1841C	10,281	150.00	175.00	300.00
1841D	4,164	175.00	250.00	350.00
1842	2,823	175.00	250.00	350.00
1842C	6,729	150.00	175.00	275.00
1842D	4,643	150.00	175.00	325.00
1842O	19,800	75.00	100.00	175.00
1843	100,546	75.00	100.00	140.00
1843C Large or small date	26,064	100.00	150.00	225.00
1843D Small date	36,209	100.00	150.00	225.00
1843O Large date	} 368,002	75.00	100.00	150.00
1843O Small date		75.00	100.00	150.00
1844	6,784	150.00	175.00	275.00
1844C	11,622	100.00	150.00	225.00
1844D	17,332	100.00	150.00	225.00
1845	91,051	75.00	100.00	140.00
1845D	19,460	100.00	150.00	225.00
1845O	4,000	150.00	250.00	385.00
1846	21,598	75.00	100.00	150.00
1846C	4,808	150.00	250.00	375.00
1846D	19,303	125.00	175.00	300.00
1846O	62,000	75.00	100.00	150.00
1847	29,814	75.00	100.00	140.00
1847C	23,226	100.00	150.00	225.00
1847D	15,784	100.00	150.00	250.00

QUARTER EAGLES ($2.50 Gold Pieces)

CALIF. GOLD QUARTER EAGLE

In 1848 about two hundred and thirty ounces of gold were sent to Secretary of War Marcy by Col. R. B. Mason, Military Governor of California. The gold was turned over to the mint and made into quarter eagles. The distinguishing mark "CAL." was punched above the eagle on the reverse side, while the coins were in the die.

	Quan. Minted	Fine	V. Fine	Ex. Fine
1847O	124,000	$75.00	$100.00	$140.00
1848	7,497	250.00	325.00	550.00
1848 CAL. over eagle	1,389	2,300	3,100	5,000
1848C	16,788	120.00	175.00	275.00
1848D	13,771	125.00	190.00	300.00
1849	23,294	75.00	100.00	140.00
1849C	10,220	120.00	175.00	300.00
1849D	10,945	120.00	175.00	300.00
1850	252,923	75.00	100.00	140.00
1850C	9,148	125.00	190.00	300.00
1850D	12,148	125.00	190.00	300.00
1850O	84,000	75.00	100.00	140.00
1851	1,372,748	75.00	100.00	140.00
1851C	14,923	125.00	190.00	300.00
1851D	11,264	125.00	190.00	300.00
1851O	148,000	75.00	100.00	140.00
1852	1,159,681	75.00	100.00	140.00
1852C	9,772	125.00	190.00	300.00
1852D	4,078	150.00	220.00	350.00
1852O	140,000	75.00	100.00	140.00
1853	1,404,668	75.00	100.00	140.00
1853D	3,178	240.00	375.00	600.00
1854	596,258	75.00	100.00	140.00
1854C	7,295	120.00	175.00	275.00
1854D	1,760	1,000	1,200	2,000
1854O	153,000	75.00	100.00	140.00
1854S	246			——
1855	235,480	75.00	100.00	140.00
1855C	3,677	275.00	450.00	700.00
1855D	1,123	600.00	850.00	1,400
1856	384,240	75.00	100.00	140.00
1856C	7,913	120.00	175.00	300.00
1856D	874	950.00	1,400	3,000
1856O	21,100	75.00	100.00	140.00
1856S	71,120	75.00	100.00	140.00
1857	214,130	75.00	100.00	140.00
1857D	2,364	225.00	375.00	550.00
1857O	34,000	75.00	100.00	140.00
1857S	69,200	75.00	100.00	140.00
1858	47,377	75.00	100.00	140.00
1858C	9,056	120.00	175.00	275.00
1859	39,444	75.00	100.00	140.00

QUARTER EAGLES ($2.50 Gold Pieces)

	Quan. Minted	Fine	V. Fine	Ex. Fine
1859D	2,244	$200.00	$300.00	$550.00
1859S	15,200	75.00	100.00	140.00
1860	22,675	75.00	100.00	140.00
1860C	7,469	110.00	165.00	300.00
1860S	35,600	75.00	100.00	150.00
1861	1,238,878	75.00	100.00	140.00
1861S	24,000	75.00	100.00	150.00
1862	98,543	75.00	100.00	140.00
1862S	8,000	100.00	125.00	200.00
1863 (Proofs only) Beware removed mint mark	30			——
1863S	10,800	75.00	100.00	140.00
1864	2,874	200.00	300.00	400.00
1865	1,545	225.00	350.00	500.00
1865S	23,376	75.00	100.00	150.00
1866	3,110	110.00	150.00	275.00
1866S	38,960	75.00	100.00	140.00
1867	3,250	110.00	150.00	250.00
1867S	28,000	75.00	100.00	140.00
1868	3,625	100.00	140.00	225.00
1868S	34,000	75.00	100.00	140.00
1869	4,345	90.00	110.00	175.00
1869S	29,500	75.00	100.00	140.00
1870	4,555	90.00	110.00	175.00
1870S	16,000	75.00	100.00	140.00
1871	5,350	90.00	110.00	175.00
1871S	22,000	75.00	100.00	140.00
1872	3,030	100.00	140.00	225.00
1872S	18,000	75.00	100.00	140.00
1873	178,025	75.00	100.00	140.00
1873S	27,000	75.00	100.00	140.00
1874	3,940	100.00	135.00	200.00
1875	420	800.00	1,350	2,750
1875S	11,600	80.00	110.00	150.00
1876	4,221	100.00	135.00	200.00
1876S	5,000	75.00	100.00	150.00
1877	1,652	200.00	250.00	375.00
1877S	35,400	75.00	100.00	140.00
1878	286,260	75.00	100.00	140.00
1878S	178,000	75.00	100.00	140.00
1879	88,990	75.00	100.00	140.00
1879S	43,500	75.00	100.00	140.00
1880	2,996	100.00	135.00	200.00
1881	691	250.00	400.00	700.00
1882	4,067	100.00	135.00	200.00
1883	2,002	110.00	140.00	200.00
1884	2,023	110.00	140.00	220.00
1885	887	200.00	325.00	500.00
1886	4,088	100.00	135.00	200.00
1887	6,282	90.00	110.00	175.00
1888	16,098	75.00	100.00	150.00
1889	17,648	75.00	100.00	150.00
1890	8,813	80.00	110.00	160.00
1891	11,004	75.00	100.00	140.00
1892	2,545	100.00	135.00	200.00

QUARTER EAGLES ($2.50 Gold Pieces)

	Quan. Minted	Fine	V. Fine	Ex. Fine
1893	30,106	$75.00	$100.00	$140.00
1894	4,122	85.00	110.00	175.00
1895	6,119	80.00	110.00	160.00
1896	19,202	75.00	100.00	140.00
1897	29,904	75.00	100.00	140.00
1898	24,165	75.00	100.00	140.00
1899	27,350	75.00	100.00	140.00
1900	67,205	75.00	100.00	140.00
1901	91,323	75.00	100.00	140.00
1902	133,733	75.00	100.00	140.00 ·
1903	201,257	75.00	100.00	140.00
1904	160,960	75.00	100.00	140.00
1905*	217,944	75.00	100.00	140.00
1906	176,490	75.00	100.00	140.00
1907	336,448	75.00	100.00	140.00

*Pieces dated 1905S are counterfeit.

INDIAN HEAD TYPE 1908-1929

This coinage represents a departure from all previous coin types. The pieces have no raised edge and the main devices and legend are incuse. Bela L. Pratt was the designer of this and the similarly executed $5.00 gold piece.

V. GOOD—*Outline of bonnet cord shows.*
FINE—*Knot in hair cord shows, but top feathers faint on wing.*
EX. FINE—*Cheekbone slightly worn. Warbonnet and headband feathers slightly worn.*

1908	565,057	70.00	90.00	120.00
1909	441,899	70.00	90.00	120.00
1910	492,682	70.00	90.00	120.00
1911	704,191	70.00	90.00	120.00
1911D	55,680	250.00	300.00	500.00
1912	616,197	70.00	90.00	120.00
1913	722,165	70.00	90.00	120.00
1914	240,117	70.00	90.00	120.00
1914D	448,000	70.00	90.00	120.00
1915	606,100	70.00	90.00	120.00
1925D	578,000	70.00	90.00	120.00
1926	446,000	70.00	90.00	120.00
1927	388,000	70.00	90.00	120.00
1928	416,000	70.00	90.00	120.00
1929	532,000	70.00	90.00	120.00

THREE-DOLLAR GOLD PIECES

(Coined from 1854 to 1889)

This denomination was authorized to facilitate postal transactions when the letter rate was made three cents. The coin was very unpopular and never circulated to any extent; when the postal rate was changed, the piece was discontinued.

All dates are of the same design; the 1870S, 1873, 1875 and 1876 are the rarest.

THREE-DOLLAR GOLD PIECES

V. GOOD—*At least 3 letters show in LIBERTY.*
FINE—*Details of curled feathers missing. Beads partly worn, but LIBERTY plain.*
EX. FINE—*Slight wear above and to right of eye, and tops of curled feathers.*

	Quan. Minted	Fine	V. Fine	Ex. Fine
1854	138,618	$240.00	$325.00	$425.00
1854D	1,120	900.00	1,500	3,000
1854O	24,000	240.00	325.00	450.00
1855	50,555	240.00	325.00	450.00
1855S	6,600	240.00	350.00	500.00
1856	26,010	240.00	350.00	450.00
1856S	34,500	240.00	350.00	475.00
1857	20,891	240.00	350.00	450.00
1857S	14,000	240.00	325.00	425.00
1858	2,133	280.00	390.00	600.00
1859	15,638	240.00	325.00	425.00
1860	7,155	240.00	325.00	450.00
1860S	7,000	240.00	325.00	475.00
1861	6,072	240.00	325.00	450.00
1862	5,785	240.00	325.00	450.00
1863	5,039	240.00	325.00	450.00
1864	2,680	275.00	350.00	500.00
1865	1,165	300.00	400.00	600.00
1866	4,030	240.00	325.00	500.00
1867	2,650	275.00	350.00	550.00
1868	4,875	240.00	325.00	500.00
1869	2,525	275.00	350.00	550.00
1870	3,535	240.00	325.00	425.00
1870S	2			Unique
1871	1,330	250.00	350.00	600.00
1872	2,030	240.00	325.00	500.00
1873 (Proofs only)	25			—
1874	41,820	240.00	325.00	425.00
1875 (Proofs only)	20			—
1876 (Proofs only)	45			—
1877	1,488	350.00	500.00	900.00
1878	82,324	240.00	325.00	425.00
1879	3,030	240.00	325.00	450.00
1880	1,036	275.00	350.00	575.00
1881	554	375.00	450.00	950.00
1882	1,576	240.00	350.00	500.00
1883	989	250.00	350.00	650.00
1884	1,106	250.00	350.00	600.00
1885	910	325.00	450.00	800.00
1886	1,142	250.00	350.00	600.00
1887	6,160	240.00	325.00	450.00
1888	5,291	240.00	325.00	450.00
1889	2,429	240.00	325.00	450.00

$4.00 GOLD OR "STELLA"

These pattern coins were first suggested by the Hon. John A. Kasson, then U.S. Minister to Austria; and it was through the efforts of Dr. W. W. Hubbell who patented the Goloid metal, used in making the Goloid Metric Dollars, that we have these beautiful and interesting pieces.

There are two distinct types in both years of issue. Barber designed the flowing hair version and Morgan the coiled hair. They were struck in gold, aluminum, copper, and white metal. Only those struck in gold are listed below.

	Quan. Minted	Proof
1879 Flowing hair	415	$15,000
1879 Coiled hair	10	——
1880 Flowing hair	15	——
1880 Coiled hair	10	——

HALF EAGLES ($5.00 Gold Pieces)
(Coined from 1795 to 1929)

Dates prior to 1807 do not bear any mark of value. 1795 to 1798 are rare; 1799 to 1814 are fairly plentiful; and those in the 1820's are all very rare and with the possible exception of 1820, 1823 and 1826, few collectors have ever owned a half eagle of that decade. The 1822 is considered the most valuable regular issue coin of the entire United States series, there being only three specimens known. Two of these are in the U.S. mint collection and therefore not available to collectors.

FINE—*Hair worn smooth but with distinct outline. After 1797 E PLURIBUS UNUM is faint but readable.*
EX. FINE—*Slight wear on hair and cheek.*

Small Eagle   Large Eagle

	Quan. Minted	Fine	Ex. Fine
1795 Small eagle	8,707	$2,000	$3,000
1795 Large eagle		3,000	6,000
1796	6,196	2,000	3,000
1797 Small eagle	3,609	2,500	6,000

HALF EAGLES ($5.00 Gold Pieces)

	Quan. Minted	Fine	Ex. Fine
1797 Large eagle		$2,000	$4,000
1798 Small eagle			
1798 Large eagle	} 24,867	550.00	900.00

1799	7,451	550.00	900.00
1800	37,628	550.00	900.00
1802 2 over 1	53,176	525.00	850.00
1803 3 over 2	33,506	525.00	850.00
1804	30,475	525.00	850.00
1805	33,183	525.00	850.00
1806	64,093	525.00	850.00
1807 Bust facing right	32,488	525.00	850.00

FINE—*LIBERTY readable but partly weak.*
EX. FINE—*Slight wear on high points of hair and curls.*

1807 Bust facing left	51,605	500.00	850.00
1808	55,578	475.00	775.00
1809	33,875	475.00	775.00
1810	100,287	475.00	775.00
1811	99,581	475.00	775.00
1812	58,087	475.00	775.00

1813	95,428	500.00	800.00
1814 over 13	15,454	600.00	1,000
1815	635		
1818	48,588	600.00	1,000
1819	51,723	5,000	14,000

HALF EAGLES ($5.00 Gold Pieces)

	Quan. Minted	Fine	Ex. Fine
1820	263,806	$600.00	$1,000
1821	34,641	1,250	4,500
1822	17,796		—
1823	14,485	900.00	2,500
1824	17,340	2,600	7,000
1825	29,060	1,400	3,500
1826	18,069	1,500	4,300
1827	24,913	2,800	7,000
1828	28,029	2,000	6,500
1829	57,442		—
1830	126,351	1,000	2,500
1831	140,594	1,000	2,500
1832	157,487	1,500	5,000
1833	193,630	1,000	2,700
1834 Motto	50,141	1,200	3,000

	Quan. Minted	Fine	Ex. Fine
1834 No motto. Plain 4	}657,460	110.00	250.00
1834 No motto. Crosslet 4		160.00	375.00
1835	371,534	110.00	260.00
1836	553,147	110.00	260.00
1837	207,121	110.00	260.00
1838	286,588	110.00	260.00
1838C	17,179	275.00	675.00
1838D	20,583	275.00	675.00

CORONET TYPE 1839-1908

Variety 1 — No motto above eagle 1839-1866

V. FINE—*LIBERTY bold. Major lines show in neck hair.*
EX. FINE—*Hair at neck sharp. Slight wear top of coronet and hair beneath.*

		V. Fine	Ex. Fine
1839	118,143	100.00	150.00
1839C	17,205	150.00	360.00
1839D	18,939	150.00	360.00
1840	137,382	100.00	135.00
1840C	18,992	135.00	350.00
1840D	22,896	135.00	350.00
1840O	40,120	120.00	175.00
1841	15,833	120.00	175.00
1841C	21,467	150.00	325.00
1841D	29,392	150.00	325.00
1841O (2 Known)	50		—
1842	27,578	100.00	150.00

HALF EAGLES ($5.00 Gold Pieces)

	Quan. Minted	V. Fine	Ex. Fine
1842C	27,432	$120.00	$250.00
1842D	59,608	120.00	250.00
1842O	16,400	110.00	175.00
1843	611,205	100.00	135.00
1843C	44,277	120.00	275.00
1843D	98,452	120.00	275.00
1843O	101,075	110.00	150.00
1844	340,330	100.00	135.00
1844C	23,631	150.00	350.00
1844D	88,982	110.00	250.00
1844O	364,600	100.00	150.00
1845	417,099	100.00	135.00
1845D	90,629	125.00	260.00
1845O	41,000	100.00	200.00
1846	395,942	100.00	135.00
1846C	12,995	150.00	375.00
1846D	80,294	110.00	250.00
1846O	58,000	100.00	175.00
1847	915,981	100.00	135.00
1847C	84,151	130.00	275.00
1847D	64,405	130.00	275.00
1847O	12,000	130.00	275.00
1848	260,775	100.00	135.00
1848C	64,472	130.00	275.00
1848D	47,465	130.00	275.00
1849	133,070	100.00	135.00
1849C	64,823	150.00	275.00
1849D	39,036	150.00	275.00
1850	64,491	100.00	135.00
1850C	63,591	130.00	275.00
1850D	43,984	130.00	275.00
1851	377,505	100.00	135.00
1851C	49,176	130.00	275.00
1851D	62,710	130.00	275.00
1851O	41,000	110.00	200.00
1852	573,901	100.00	135.00
1852C	72,574	130.00	275.00
1852D	91,584	130.00	275.00
1853	305,770	100.00	135.00
1853C	65,571	130.00	275.00
1853D	89,678	130.00	275.00
1854	160,675	100.00	135.00
1854C	39,283	130.00	275.00
1854D	56,413	130.00	275.00
1854O	46,000	110.00	200.00
1854S	268	—	—
1855	117,098	100.00	135.00
1855C	39,788	130.00	275.00
1855D	22,432	130.00	275.00
1855O	11,100	140.00	290.00
1855S	61,000	100.00	150.00
1856	197,990	100.00	135.00
1856C	28,457	130.00	275.00
1856D	19,786	130.00	275.00

HALF EAGLES ($5.00 Gold Pieces)

	Quan. Minted	V. Fine	Ex. Fine
1856O	10,000	$175.00	$425.00
1856S	105,100	100.00	150.00
1857	98,188	100.00	135.00
1857C	31,360	150.00	285.00
1857D	17,046	150.00	285.00
1857O	13,000	150.00	285.00
1857S	87,000	100.00	140.00
1858	15,136	110.00	175.00
1858C	38,856	125.00	250.00
1858D	15,362	125.00	275.00
1858S	18,600	110.00	210.00
1859	16,814	100.00	140.00
1859C	31,847	110.00	250.00
1859D	10,366	150.00	400.00
1959S	13,220	110.00	250.00
1860	19,825	100.00	150.00
1860C	14,813	140.00	325.00
1860D	14,635	140.00	325.00
1860S	21,200	120.00	200.00
1861	688,150	100.00	135.00
1861C	6,879	600.00	1,400
1861D	1,597	1,900	3,250
1861S	18,000	110.00	200.00
1862	4,465	175.00	350.00
1862S	9,500	110.00	250.00
1863	2,472	225.00	450.00
1863S	17,000	100.00	135.00
1864	4,220	175.00	300.00
1864S	3,888	550.00	1,300
1865	1,295	200.00	400.00
1865S	27,612	110.00	200.00
1866S No motto	9,000	115.00	300.00

Variety 2 — Motto above eagle 1866-1908

V. FINE—*IN GOD WE TRUST complete. Hair curls worn but evident.*

EX. FINE—*Slight wear on hair at top of head, below "L" in LIBERTY, top of coronet, and on reverse, upper wings and neck of eagle.*

1866 Motto	6,730	150.00	325.00
1866S Motto	34,920	110.00	275.00
1867	6,920	110.00	275.00
1867S	29,000	110.00	200.00
1868	5,725	120.00	250.00
1868S	52,000	100.00	150.00
1869	1,785	250.00	500.00
1869S	31,000	100.00	150.00
1870	4,035	120.00	260.00
1870CC	7,675	800.00	1,600
1870S	17,000	110.00	175.00

HALF EAGLES ($5.00 Gold Pieces)

	Quan. Minted	V. Fine	Ex. Fine
1871	3,230	$160.00	$300.00
1871CC	20,770	190.00	325.00
1871S	25,000	110.00	185.00
1872	1,690	250.00	600.00
1872CC	16,980	250.00	600.00
1872S	36,400	100.00	140.00
1873	112,505	100.00	135.00
1873CC	7,416	225.00	600.00
1873S	31,000	100.00	135.00
1874	3,508	175.00	300.00
1874CC	21,198	120.00	275.00
1874S	16,000	110.00	175.00
1875	220		——
1875CC	11,828	170.00	375.00
1875S	9,000	110.00	250.00
1876	1,477	325.00	800.00
1876CC	6,887	250.00	500.00
1876S	4,000	250.00	500.00
1877	1,152	300.00	700.00
1877CC	8,680	260.00	550.00
1877S	26,700	100.00	135.00
1878	131,740	100.00	125.00
1878CC	9,054	410.00	1,100
1878S	144,700	100.00	125.00
1879	301,950	100.00	125.00
1879CC	17,281	120.00	250.00
1879S	426,200	100.00	125.00
1880	3,166,436	100.00	125.00
1880CC	51,017	110.00	150.00
1880S	1,348,900	100.00	125.00
1881	5,708,802	100.00	125.00
1881CC	13,886	110.00	170.00
1881S	969,000	100.00	125.00
1882	2,514,568	100.00	125.00
1882CC	82,817	110.00	150.00
1882S	969,000	100.00	125.00
1883	233,461	100.00	125.00
1883CC	12,958	110.00	150.00
1883S	83,200	100.00	125.00
1884	191,078	100.00	125.00
1884CC	16,402	110.00	175.00
1884S	177,000	100.00	125.00
1885	601,506	100.00	125.00
1885S	1,211,500	100.00	125.00
1886	388,432	100.00	125.00
1886S	3,268,000	100.00	125.00
1887 (Proofs only) Beware removed mint mark	87	Proof	10,000
1887S	1,912,000	100.00	125.00
1888	18,296	100.00	130.00
1888S	293,900	100.00	125.00
1889	7,565	175.00	250.00
1890	4,328	200.00	275.00
1890CC	53,800	110.00	140.00
1891	61,413	100.00	130.00

HALF EAGLES ($5.00 Gold Pieces)

	Quan. Minted	V. Fine	Ex. Fine
1891CC	208,000	$110.00	$130.00
1892	753,572	100.00	125.00
1892CC	82,968	110.00	140.00
1892O	10,000	350.00	600.00
1892S	298,400	100.00	125.00
1893	1,528,197	100.00	125.00
1893CC	60,000	110.00	140.00
1893O	110,000	110.00	150.00
1893S	224,000	100.00	125.00
1894	957,955	100.00	125.00
1894O	16,600	120.00	200.00
1894S	55,900	100.00	125.00
1895	1,345,936	100.00	125.00
1895S	112,000	100.00	125.00
1896	59,063	100.00	125.00
1896S	155,400	100.00	125.00
1897	867,883	100.00	125.00
1897S	354,000	100.00	125.00
1898	633,495	100.00	125.00
1898S	1,397,400	100.00	125.00
1899	1,710,729	100.00	125.00
1899S	1,545,000	100.00	125.00
1900	1,405,730	100.00	125.00
1900S	329,000	100.00	125.00
1901	616,040	100.00	125.00
1901S	3,648,000	100.00	125.00
1902	172,562	100.00	125.00
1902S	939,000	100.00	125.00
1903	227,024	100.00	125.00
1903S	1,855,000	100.00	125.00
1904	392,136	100.00	125.00
1904S	97,000	100.00	125.00
1905	302,308	100.00	125.00
1905S	880,700	100.00	125.00
1906	348,820	100.00	125.00
1906D	320,000	100.00	125.00
1906S	598,000	100.00	125.00
1907	626,192	100.00	125.00
1907D	888,000	100.00	125.00
1908 Liberty head	421,874	100.00	125.00

INDIAN HEAD TYPE 1908-1929

This type conforms to the $2.50 gold piece of the same design and date span. The incuse designs and lettering make these coins a unique series in our United States coinage.

Values shown
are for pieces with
well struck
mint marks

V. FINE—*Noticeable wear on large middle feathers and tip of eagle's wing.*
EX. FINE—*Slight wear on cheekbone and jawbone beneath. Top feathers on wing outlined but worn.*

HALF EAGLES ($5.00 Gold Pieces)

	Quan. Minted	V. Fine	Ex. Fine
1908 Indian head	578,012	$120.00	$150.00
1908D	148,000	120.00	150.00
1908S	82,000	150.00	300.00
1909	627,138	120.00	150.00
1909D	3,423,560	120.00	150.00
1909O (Beware of altered mint mark)	34,200	210.00	375.00
1909S	297,200	120.00	150.00
1910	604,250	120.00	150.00
1910D	193,600	120.00	150.00
1910S	770,200	120.00	150.00
1911	915,139	120.00	150.00
1911D	72,500	150.00	175.00
1911S	1,416,000	120.00	150.00
1912	790,144	120.00	150.00
1912S	392,000	120.00	150.00
1913	916,099	120.00	150.00
1913S	408,000	120.00	150.00
1914	247,125	120.00	150.00
1914D	247,000	120.00	150.00
1914S	263,000	120.00	150.00
1915	588,075	120.00	150.00
1915S	164,000	120.00	150.00
1916S	240,000	120.00	150.00
1929	662,000	1,500	2,000

Values shown are for pieces with well struck mint marks

EAGLES ($10.00 Gold Pieces)

(Coined from 1795 to 1933; none coined between 1805 and 1837)

Although coinage extended over a long period there are only a few major types with some minor variations such as the number of stars in the first type. The Liberty head was adopted in 1838 and coined until 1907, a motto being added on the reverse in 1866; the Indian head type was introduced in 1907.

CAPPED BUST TO RIGHT, SMALL EAGLE 1795-1797

FINE—*Details on turban and head obliterated.*
EX. FINE—*Noticeable wear points are: hair left of eye, strand which sweeps across turban and eagle's wingtips.*

		Fine	Ex. Fine
1795	5,583	2,000	4,500
1796	4,146	2,000	4,500
1797 Small eagle	2,466	2,400	7,000

EAGLES ($10.00 Gold Pieces)
CAPPED BUST TO RIGHT, HERALDIC EAGLE 1797-1804

	Quan. Minted	Fine	Ex. Fine
1797 Large eagle	12,089	$1,200	$2,400
1798 Over 97. 4 stars facing	900	2,500	6,000
1798 Over 97. 6 stars facing	842	5,000	——
1799	37,449	900.00	2,000
1800	5,999	1,100	2,200
1801	44,344	900.00	2,000
1803	15,017	1,100	2,200
1804	3,757	1,400	3,500

CORONET TYPE 1838-1907
Variety 1 — No motto above eagle 1838-1866

V. FINE—*Hairlines above coronet worn. Curls under ear worn but defined.*

EX. FINE—*Wear shows at top of head, hair below "L" in LIBERTY, top of coronet, upper part of wings and neck of eagle.*

		V. Fine	Ex. Fine
1838	7,200	425.00	925.00
1839	38,248	300.00	600.00
1840	47,338	150.00	165.00
1841	63,131	150.00	165.00
1841O	2,500	300.00	700.00
1842	81,507	150.00	165.00
1842O	27,400	160.00	180.00
1843	75,462	150.00	165.00
1843O	175,162	150.00	165.00
1844	6,361	250.00	425.00
1844O	118,700	150.00	165.00
1845	26,153	150.00	165.00
1845O	47,500	150.00	165.00
1846	20,095	150.00	165.00
1846O	81,780	150.00	165.00
1847	862,258	150.00	165.00
1847O	571,500	150.00	165.00
1848	145,484	150.00	165.00
1848O	35,850	150.00	165.00
1849	653,618	150.00	165.00
1849O	23,900	160.00	200.00
1850	291,451	150.00	165.00

EAGLES ($10.00 Gold Pieces)

	Quan. Minted	V. Fine	Ex. Fine
1850O	57,500	$150.00	$165.00
1851	176,328	150.00	165.00
1851O	263,000	150.00	165.00
1852	263,106	150.00	165.00
1852O	18,000	160.00	175.00
1853	201,253	150.00	165.00
1853O	51,000	150.00	165.00
1854	54,250	150.00	165.00
1854O	52,500	160.00	175.00
1854S	123,826	150.00	175.00
1855	121,701	150.00	165.00
1855O	18,000	170.00	200.00
1855S	9,000	190.00	400.00
1856	60,490	150.00	165.00
1856O	14,500	150.00	175.00
1856S	68,000	150.00	175.00
1857	16,606	150.00	175.00
1857O	5,500	230.00	575.00
1857S	26,000	150.00	175.00
1858 (Beware removed mint mark)	2,521	2,200	4,500
1858O	20,000	150.00	175.00
1858S	11,800	150.00	175.00
1859	16,093	150.00	175.00
1859O	2,300	500.00	950.00
1859S	7,000	230.00	550.00
1860	15,105	150.00	175.00
1860O	11,100	150.00	175.00
1860S	5,000	280.00	550.00
1861	113,233	150.00	165.00
1861S	15,500	150.00	175.00
1862	10,995	160.00	200.00
1862S	12,500	160.00	200.00
1863	1,248	1,000	2,000
1863S	10,000	175.00	400.00
1864	3,580	350.00	750.00
1864S	2,500	1,000	1,900
1865	4,005	400.00	750.00
1865S	16,700	340.00	650.00
1866S No motto (All Kinds)	20,000	350.00	750.00

Values listed for all gold coins are for choice specimens. Those grading less than the conditions listed bring proportionately less.

Variety 2 — Motto above eagle 1866-1907

V. FINE—*Half of hairlines over coronet visible. Curls under ear worn but defined. IN GOD WE TRUST and its ribbon are sharp.*

EX. FINE—*Wear shows at top of head, hair below "L" in LIBERTY, top of coronet, upper part of wings and neck of eagle.*

1866	3,780	180.00	500.00
1866S With motto		175.00	350.00
1867	3,140	175.00	450.00
1867S	9,000	175.00	350.00
1868	10,655	150.00	175.00

EAGLES ($10.00 Gold Pieces)

	Quan. Minted	V. Fine	Ex. Fine
1868S	13,500	$160.00	$175.00
1869	1,855	300.00	800.00
1869S	6,430	190.00	450.00
1870	4,025	230.00	450.00
1870CC	5,908	900.00	1,700
1870S	8,000	175.00	415.00
1871	1,820	300.00	800.00
1871CC	8,085	300.00	750.00
1871S	16,500	170.00	220.00
1872	1,650	300.00	800.00
1872CC	4,600	300.00	750.00
1872S	17,300	160.00	200.00
1873	825	1,000	2,300
1873CC	4,543	550.00	1,500
1873S	12,000	160.00	225.00
1874	53,160	150.00	165.00
1874CC	16,767	175.00	300.00
1874S	10,000	160.00	250.00
1875	120	—	—
1875CC	7,715	250.00	600.00
1876	732	1,000	1,700
1876CC	4,696	275.00	700.00
1876S	5,000	220.00	500.00
1877	817	1,000	1,800
1877CC	3,332	340.00	800.00
1877S	17,000	150.00	165.00
1878	73,800	150.00	165.00
1878CC	3,244	410.00	950.00
1878S	26,100	150.00	165.00
1879	384,770	150.00	165.00
1879CC	1,762	1,800	3,250
1879O	1,500	700.00	1,300
1879S	224,000	150.00	165.00
1880	1,644,876	150.00	165.00
1880CC	11,190	150.00	175.00
1880O	9,200	150.00	185.00
1880S	506,250	450.00	165.00
1881	3,877,260	150.00	165.00
1881CC	24,015	150.00	175.00
1881O	8,350	150.00	185.00
1881S	970,000	150.00	165.00
1882	2,324,480	150.00	165.00
1882CC	6,764	175.00	275.00
1882O	10,820	150.00	165.00
1882S	132,000	150.00	165.00
1883	208,740	150.00	165.00
1883CC	12,000	160.00	200.00
1883O	800	1,300	2,600
1883S	38,000	150.00	165.00
1884	76,905	150.00	165.00
1884CC	9,925	150.00	200.00
1884S	124,250	150.00	165.00
1885	253,527	150.00	165.00
1885S	228,000	150.00	165.00
1886	236,160	150.00	165.00

EAGLES ($10.00 Gold Pieces)

	Quan. Minted	V. Fine	Ex. Fine
1886S	826,000	$150.00	$165.00
1887	53,680	150.00	165.00
1887S	817,000	150.00	165.00
1888	132,996	150.00	165.00
1888O	21,335	150.00	185.00
1888S	648,700	150.00	165.00
1889	4,485	175.00	400.00
1889S	425,400	150.00	165.00
1890	58,043	150.00	165.00
1890CC	17,500	160.00	190.00
1891	91,868	150.00	165.00
1891CC	103,732	150.00	165.00
1892	797,552	150.00	165.00
1892CC	40,000	160.00	175.00
1892O	28,688	150.00	165.00
1892S	115,500	150.00	165.00
1893	1,840,895	150.00	165.00
1893CC	14,000	150.00	200.00
1893O	17,000	150.00	180.00
1893S	141,350	150.00	165.00
1894	2,470,778	150.00	165.00
1894O	107,500	150.00	165.00
1894S	25,000	150.00	175.00
1895	567,826	150.00	165.00
1895O	98,000	150.00	165.00
1895S	49,000	150.00	165.00
1896	76,348	150.00	165.00
1896S	123,750	150.00	165.00
1897	1,000,159	150.00	165.00
1897O	42.500	150.00	165.00
1897S	234,750	150.00	165.00
1898	812,197	150.00	165.00
1898S	473,600	150.00	165.00
1899	1,262,305	150.00	165.00
1899O	37,047	150.00	165.00
1899S	841,000	150.00	165.00
1900	293,960	150.00	165.00
1900S	81,000	150.00	165.00
1901	1,718,825	150.00	165.00
1901O	72,041	150.00	165.00
1901S	2,812,750	150.00	165.00
1902	82,513	150.00	165.00
1902S	469,500	150.00	165.00
1903	125,926	150.00	165.00
1903O	112,771	150.00	165.00
1903S	538,000	150.00	165.00
1904	162,038	150.00	165.00
1904O	108,950	150.00	165.00
1905	201,078	150.00	165.00
1905S	369,250	151.00	165.00
1906	165,497	150.00	165.00
1906D	981,000	150.00	165.00
1906O	86,895	150.00	165.00
1906S	457,000	150.00	165.00
1907 Liberty head	1,203,973	150.00	165.00

EAGLES ($10.00 Gold Pieces)

	Quan. Minted	V. Fine	Ex. Fine
1907D Liberty	1,030,000	$150.00	$165.00
1907S Liberty	210,500	150.00	165.00

INDIAN HEAD TYPE 1907-1933

Augustus Saint-Gaudens, perhaps the greatest of modern sculptors, introduced a new high standard of art in United States coins with his $10.00 and $20.00 gold coin designs of 1907. The eagle ($10) shows Liberty with an Indian war bonnet, while a majestic American eagle dominates the reverse.

Variety 1 — No motto on reverse 1907-1908

V. FINE — *Bonnet feathers worn near band. Hair high points show wear.*

EX. FINE — *Trace of wear on cheekbone, feathers on headdress, above eagle's eye and left wing.*

	Quan. Minted	V. Fine	Ex. Fine
1907 Indian, "wire edge," periods before and after legends	500	1,700	2,700
1907 Rounded edge, with periods	42	—	—
1907 No periods	239,406	250.00	275.00
1908 No motto to left of eagle	33,500	265.00	300.00
1908D No motto	210,000	250.00	275.00

Variety 2 — Motto on reverse 1908-1933

	Quan. Minted	V. Fine	Ex. Fine
1908 Motto "In God We Trust" added	341,486	250.00	275.00
1908D Motto	836,500	250.00	275.00
1908S Motto	59,853	265.00	300.00
1909	184,860	250.00	275.00
1909D	121,540	250.00	275.00
1909S	292,350	250.00	275.00
1910	318,704	250.00	275.00
1910D	2,356,640	250.00	275.00
1910S	811,000	250.00	275.00
1911	505,595	250.00	275.00
1911D	30,100	275.00	325.00
1911S	51,000	250.00	290.00
1912	405,083	250.00	275.00
1912S	300,000	250.00	275.00
1913	442,071	250.00	275.00
1913S	66,000	250.00	275.00
1914	151,050	250.00	275.00
1914D	343,500	250.00	275.00
1914S	208,000	250.00	275.00
1915	351,075	250.00	275.00
1915S	59,000	250.00	290.00
1916S	138,500	250.00	290.00
1920S	126,500	2,800	6,000
1926	1,014,000	250.00	275.00
1930S	96,000	2,000	3,000
1932	4,463,000	250.00	275.00
1933	312,500	—	—

DOUBLE EAGLES ($20.00 Gold Pieces)

(Coined for general circulation from 1850 through 1932)

This series is not collected extensively by dates except by the more wealthy collectors due to the high face value. Most of the dates are not rare except in uncirculated or proof condition; 1883 is the rarest date as only 40 were coined. Proofs before 1890 are quite rare as only 25 to 35 pieces each year were struck for collectors. The last year of coinage, 1933, was not officially released.

CORONET TYPE 1849-1907

V. FINE — *LIBERTY is bold. Jewels on crown defined. Hair worn above ear.*
EX. FINE — *Slight wear on curls and crown jewels. Tiny bagmarks.*

		Quan. Minted	V. Fine	Ex. Fine
1849 (In U. S. Mint Collection)		1		
1850		1,170,261	$300.00	$350.00
1850O		141,000	300.00	475.00
1851		2,087,155	280.00	300.00
1851O		315,000	300.00	350.00
1852		2,053,026	280.00	300.00
1852O		190,000	300.00	365.00
1853		1,261,326	280.00	300.00
1853O		71,000	325.00	500.00
1854		757,899	280.00	300.00
1854O		3,250	—	—
1854S		141,468	300.00	440.00
1855		364,666	280.00	300.00
1855O	Values listed for all gold coins	8,000	1,200	2,000
1855S	are for choice specimens.	879,675	280.00	300.00
1856	Those grading less than the	329,878	280.00	300.00
1856O	conditions listed bring pro-	2,250	4,000	—
1856S	portionately less.	1,189,750	280.00	300.00
1857		439,375	280.00	300.00
1857O		30,000	450.00	700.00
1857S		970,500	280.00	300.00
1858		211,714	280.00	300.00
1858O		35,250	450.00	700.00
1858S		846,710	280.00	300.00
1859		43,597	280.00	300.00
1859O		9,100	1,200	2,000
1859S		636,445	280.00	300.00
1860		577,670	280.00	300.00
1860O		6,600	1,600	2,400
1860S		544,950	280.00	300.00
1861		2,976,453	280.00	300.00
1861O		17,741	900.00	1,500

DOUBLE EAGLES ($20.00 Gold Pieces)

	Quan. Minted	V. Fine	Ex. Fine
1861S	768,000	$280.00	$300.00
1862	92,133	325.00	500.00
1862S	854,173	280.00	300.00
1863	142,790	280.00	300.00
1863S	966,570	280.00	300.00
1864	204,285	280.00	300.00
1864S	793,660	280.00	300.00
1865	351,200	280.00	300.00
1865S	1,042,500	280.00	300.00
1866S No motto		400.00	650.00
1866 Motto	698,775	280.00	300.00
1866S Motto	(all kinds) 842,250	280.00	300.00
1867	251,065	280.00	300.00
1867S	920,750	280.00	300.00
1868	98,600	300.00	350.00
1868S	837,500	280.00	300.00
1869	175,155	280.00	300.00
1869S	686,750	280.00	300.00
1870	155,185	280.00	300.00
1870CC	3,789	——	——
1870S	982,000	280.00	300.00
1871	80,150	280.00	300.00
1871CC	17,387	950.00	1,500
1871S	928,000	280.00	300.00
1872	251,880	280.00	300.00
1872CC	26,900	400.00	550.00
1872S	780,000	280.00	300.00
1873	1,709,825	280.00	300.00
1873CC	22,410	410.00	600.00
1873S	1,040,600	280.00	300.00
1874	366,800	280.00	300.00
1874CC	115,085	300.00	350.00
1874S	1,214,000	280.00	300.00
1875	295,740	280.00	300.00
1875CC	111,151	280.00	300.00
1875S	1,230.000	280.00	300.00
1876	583,905	280.00	300.00
1876CC	138,441	280.00	300.00
1876S	1,597,000	280.00	300.00
1877	397,670	280.00	300.00
1877CC	42,565	280.00	300.00
1877S	1,735,000	280.00	300.00
1878	543,645	280.00	300.00
1878CC	13,180	400.00	500.00
1878S	1,739,000	280.00	300.00
1879	207,630	280.00	300.00
1879CC	10,708	500.00	750.00
1879O	2,325	1,900	3,200
1879S	1,223,800	280.00	300.00
1880	51,456	280.00	300.00
1880S	836,000	280.00	300.00
1881	2,260	2,100	3,500
1881S	727,000	280.00	300.00
1882	630	3,800	7,000
1882CC	39,140	300.00	350.00

DOUBLE EAGLES ($20.00 Gold Pieces)

	Quan. Minted	V. Fine	Ex. Fine
1882S	1,125,000	$280.00	$300.00
1883 (Proofs only) Beware removed mint mark	40		——
1883CC	59,962	300.00	350.00
1883S	1,189,000	280.00	300.00
1884 (Proofs only) Beware removed mint mark	71		——
1884CC	81,139	300.00	350.00
1884S	916,000	280.00	300.00
1885	828	3,000	4,250
1885CC	9,450	450.00	600.00
1885S	683,500	280.00	300.00
1886	1,106	3,200	6,000
1887 (Proofs only) Beware removed mint mark	121		——
1887S	283,000	280.00	300.00
1888	226,266	280.00	300.00
1888S	859,600	280.00	300.00
1889	44,111	280.00	300.00
1889CC	30,945	300.00	350.00
1889S	774,700	280.00	300.00
1890	75,995	280.00	300.00
1890CC	91,209	280.00	300.00
1890S	802,750	280.00	300.00
1891	1,442	1,400	2,300
1891CC	5,000	700.00	1,400
1891S	1,288,125	280.00	300.00
1892	4,523	800.00	1,300
1892CC	27,265	300.00	350.00
1892S	930,150	280.00	300.00
1893	344,339	280.00	300.00
1893CC	18,402	350.00	410.00
1893S	996,175	280.00	300.00
1894	1,368,990	280.00	300.00
1894S	1,048,550	280.00	300.00
1895	1,114,656	280.00	300.00
1895S	1,143,500	280.00	300.00
1896	792,663	280.00	300.00
1896S	1,403,925	280.00	300.00
1897	1,383,261	280.00	300.00
1897S	1,470,250	280.00	300.00
1898	170,470	280.00	300.00
1898S	2,575,175	280.00	300.00
1899	1,699,384	280.00	300.00
1899S	2,010,300	280.00	300.00
1900	1,874,584	280.00	300.00
1900S	2,459,500	280.00	300.00
1901	111,526	280.00	300.00
1901S	1,596,000	280.00	300.00
1902	31,254	280.00	300.00
1902S	1,753,625	280.00	300.00
1903	287,428	280.00	300.00
1903S	954,000	280.00	300.00
1904	6,256,797	280.00	300.00
1904S	5,134,175	280.00	300.00
1905	59,011	280.00	300.00
1905S	1,813,000	280.00	300.00
1906	69,690	300.00	350.00

DOUBLE EAGLES ($20.00 Gold Pieces)

	Quan. Minted	V Fine	Ex. Fine
1906D	620,250	$280.00	$300.00
1906S	2,065,750	280.00	300.00
1907 Liberty	1,451,864	280.00	300.00
1907D Liberty	842,250	280.00	300.00
1907S Liberty	2,165,800	280.00	300.00

SAINT-GAUDENS TYPE 1907-1933

This design by Augustus Saint-Gaudens is universally acclaimed as one of the most beautiful of all United States coinages.

V. FINE — *Wear evident on right leg. Eagle's wing tips worn slightly.*
EX. FINE — *Drapery lines on chest visible. Wear on right breast, knee and below. Eagle's feathers on breast and right wing are bold.*

1907 Flying eagle, MCMVII	11,250	950.00	1,700
1907 Flying eagle, 1907	361,667	280.00	300.00
1908 No motto below eagle	4,271,551	280.00	300.00
1908D No motto	663,750	280.00.	300.00
1908 Motto (In God We Trust)	156,359	280.00	300.00
1908D Motto	349,500	280.00	300.00
1908S Motto	22,000	350.00	425.00
1909 9 over 8	⎰161,282	300.00	350.00
1909 Normal date	⎱	280.00	300.00
1909D	52,500	350.00	480.00
1909S	2,744,925	280.00	300.00
1910	482,167	280.00	300.00
1910D	429,000	280.00	300.00
1910S	2,128,250	280.00	300.00
1911	197,350	280.00	300.00
1911D	846,500	280.00	300.00
1911S	775,750	280.00	300.00
1912	149,824	280.00	300.00
1913	168,838	280.00	300.00
1913D	393,500	280.00	300.00
1913S	34,000	300.00	350.00
1914	95,320	280.00	300.00
1914D	453,000	280.00	300.00
1914S	1,498,000	280.00	300.00
1915	152,050	280.00	300.00
1915S	567,500	280.00	300.00
1916S	796,000	280.00	300.00
1920	228,250	280.00	300.00
1920S	558,000	3,000	4,000

DOUBLE EAGLES ($20.00 Gold Pieces)

	Quan. Minted	V. Fine	Ex. Fine
1921	528,500	$4,000	$6,000
1922	1,375,500	280.00	300.00
1922S	2,658,000	280.00	300.00
1923	566,000	280.00	300.00
1923D	1,702,250	280.00	300.00
1924	4,323,500	280.00	300.00
1924D	3,049,500	350.00	400.00
1924S	2,927,500	350.00	400.00
1925	2,831,750	280.00	300.00
1925D	2,938,500	375.00	500.00
1925S	3,776,500	280.00	300.00
1926	816,750	280.00	300.00
1926D	481,000	450.00	690.00
1926S	2,041,500	300.00	350.00
1927	2,946,750	280.00	300.00
1927D	180,000	——	——
1927S	3,107,000	1,400	1,750
1928	8,816,000	280.00	300.00
1929	1,779,750	1,600	2,200
1930S	74,000	4,000	5,500
1931	2,938,250	2,200	3,400
1931D	106,500	2,500	5,000
1932	1,101,750	1,900	3,750
1933 (Not placed in circulation)	(445,550)		

COMMEMORATIVE COINS

The unique position occupied by commemoratives in United States coinage is largely because with few exceptions they are the only coins that have a real historical significance. It is this feature of commemoratives which creates interest among people who otherwise have little interest in coins.

Commemorative half dollars are considered for coinage by two committees of Congress — The Committee on Banking, Housing and Urban Affairs, and the Committee on Banking and Currency of the House. Congress is guided to a great extent by the reports of these committees when passing upon bills authorizing commemorative coins.

Memorial coins are issued either to commemorate special events, or to help pay for monuments or celebrations that commemorate historical persons, places or things.

A complete set of commemorative half dollars comprises 48 types, and with the addition of mint mark varieties makes a total of 142 coins to the series.

No commemorative coin was struck from 1940 to 1945.

COMMEMORATIVE SILVER COINS

In 1892, to commemorate the World's Columbian Exposition in Chicago, Congress authorized the coinage of a special half dollar and quarter dollar, thus starting a long line of United States commemorative coins. All commemorative coins have been distributed by private individuals or commissions; they paid the mint the fact value of the coins and in turn sold the pieces at a premium to collectors. There are a few instances in which some of the very large issues were later released to circulation at face value.

COMMEMORATIVE SILVER

Isabella, Lafayette, Alabama

The commemorative coin series is collected generally in uncirculated condition and the common varieties that have been circulated are practically unsalable. Even the rare varieties are sold at great discount when in anything but mint state.

Due to their different designs and the events they commemorate this is a popular series and is worthy of the consideration of every American collector.

Commemorative totals are given as "quantity available." In many instances a portion of the total coinage has been melted. The figures given here represent the quantity of coins that are still in the hands of collectors and dealers.

	Quan. Available	Abt. Unc.	Unc.
1893 Isabella Quarter (Columbian Exposition).............	24,214	$120.00	$275.00

| 1900 Lafayette Dollar................................. | 36,026 | 210.00 | 900.00 |

HALF DOLLARS
(Listed alphabetically)

| 1921 Alabama, "2 x 2" in field........................... | 6,006 | 65.00 | 230.00 |
| 1921 Same, no "2 x 2" .... | 59,038 | 40.00 | 200.00 |

COMMEMORATIVE SILVER
Albany, Antietam, Arkansas

	Quan. Available	Abt. Unc.	Unc.
1936 Albany, New York 17,671		$92.50	$120.00

1937 Battle of Antietam 1862-1937 18,028		125.00	160.00

1935	Arkansas Centennial........................ 13,012 ⎱		
1935D	Same.. 5,505 ⎰ Set		130.00
1935S	Same.. 5,506 ⎰		
1936	Arkansas Centennial, same as 1935 —		
	date 1936 on reverse...................... 9,660 ⎱		
1936D	Same.. 9,660 ⎰ Set		115.00
1936S	Same.. 9,662 ⎰		
1937	Arkansas Centennial, same as 1935 .... 5,505 ⎱		
1937D	Same.. 5,505 ⎰ Set		150.00
1937S	Same.. 5,506 ⎰		
1938	Arkansas Centennial, same as 1935 .... 3,156 ⎱		
1938D	Same.. 3,155 ⎰ Set		250.00
1938S	Same.. 3,156 ⎰		
1939	Arkansas, same as 1935.................... 2,104 ⎱		
1939D	Same.. 2,104 ⎰ Set		750.00
1939S	Same.. 2,105 ⎰		
	Single type coin		22.00	32.00

COMMEMORATIVE SILVER

Bay Bridge, Boone

		Quan. Available	Abt. Unc.	Unc.
1936S	San Francisco-Oakland Bay Bridge..........	71,424	$32.00	$40.00

1934	Daniel Boone Bicentennial..................	10,007		35.00	52.50
1935	Same	10,010			
1935D	Same	5,005	Set		125.00
1935S	Same	5,005			

1935	Daniel Boone Bicentennial, same as 1934 but small 1934 added on reverse	10,008			
1935D	Same	2,003	Set		750.00
1935S	Same	2,004			
1936	D. Boone Bicentennial, same as 1934	12,012			
1936D	Same	5,005	Set		120.00
1936S	Same	5,006			
1937	D. Boone Bicentennial, same as 1934	9,810			
1937D	Same	2,506	Set		325.00
1937S	Same	2,506			
1938	Daniel Boone, same as 1934	2,100			
1938D	Same	2,100	Set		600.00
1938S	Same	2,100			
	Single type coin...................................			21.00	37.00

COMMEMORATIVE SILVER
Bridgeport, California, Cincinnati, Cleveland

	Quan. Available	Abt. Unc.	Unc.
1936 Bridgeport, Conn., Centennial................... 25,015		$42.00	$70.00

1925S California Diamond Jubilee 86,594		35.00	63.00

1936 Cincinnati Music Center..................... 5,005	Set		
1936D Same 5,005			600.00
1936S Same 5,006			
Single type coin..................................		120.00	200.00

1936 Cleveland, Great Lakes Exposition 50,030		20.00	30.00

COMMEMORATIVE SILVER
Columbia, S.C., Columbian, Connecticut, Delaware

		Quan. Available	Abt. Unc.	Unc.
1936	Columbia, S.C., Sesquicentennial	9,007		
1936D	Same	8,009 } Set		$425.00
1936S	Same	8,007		
	Single type coin.		$75.00	125.00

1892	Columbian Exposition	950,000	4.00	12.50
1893	Same	1,550,405	4.00	12.50

1935	Connecticut Tercentenary	25,018	85.00	110.00

1936	Deleware Tercentenary	20,993	80.00	95.00

COMMEMORATIVE SILVER
Elgin, Gettysburg, Grant, Hawaiian

		Quan. Available	Abt. Unc.	Unc.
1936	Elgin, Illinois, Centennial	20,015	$60.00	$95.00

| 1936 | Battle of Gettysburg 1863-1938 | 26,928 | 75.00 | 130.00 |

1922 Grant Memorial, small star above word
"Grant" in obv. field............................ 4,256   200.00   375.00
(Fake stars have flattened spot on reverse.)
1922 Same, no star in obverse field.................... 67,405   26.00   52.50

1928 Hawaiian Sesquicentennial 10,008   470.00   800.00

COMMEMORATIVE SILVER
Hudson, Huguenot, Iowa, Lexington

	Quan. Available	Abt. Unc.	Unc.
1935 Hudson N. Y. Sesquicentennial 10,008		$310.00	$400.00

| 1924 Huguenot-Walloon Tercentenary .... 142,080 | 32.50 | 50.00 |

| 1946 Iowa Centennial .... 100,057 | 25.00 | 31.00 |

| 1925 Lexington-Concord Sesquicentennial................ 162,013 | 22.00 | 35.00 |

COMMEMORATIVE SILVER
Lincoln, Long Island, Lynchburg, Maine

	Quan. Available	Abt. Unc.	Unc.
1918 Illinois Centennial	100,058	$25.00	$45.00

| 1936 Long Island Tercentenary | 81,826 | 23.00 | 28.00 |

| 1936 Lynchburg, Va., Sesquicentennial | 20,013 | 65.00 | 85.00 |

| 1920 Maine Centennial | 50,028 | 30.00 | 60.00 |

COMMEMORATIVE SILVER
Maryland, Missouri, Monroe, New Rochelle

	Quan. Available	Abt. Unc.	Unc.
1934 Maryland Tercentenary 25,015		$57.50	$75.00

1921 Missouri Centennial, "2 ★ 4" above "1821"........... 5,000		150.00	450.00
1921 Same, no "2 ★ 4"................................. 15,428		150.00	450.00

1923S Monroe Doctrine Centennial..................... 274,077		12.00	25.00

1938 New Rochelle, N. Y. 1688-1938..................... 15,266		120.00	170.00

COMMEMORATIVE SILVER
Norfolk, Oregon, Panama-Pacific

		Quan Available	Abt. Unc.	Unc.
1936	Norfolk, Va., Bicentennial	16,936	$110.00	$150.00

1926	Oregon Trail Memorial	47,955	30.00	60.00
1926S	Same	83,055	30.00	60.00
1928	Oregon Trail Memorial, same as 1926	6,028	50.00	155.00
1933D	Oregon Trail Memorial, same	5,008	55.00	160.00
1934D	Oregon Trail Memorial, same	7,006	40.00	120.00
1936	Oregon Trail Memorial, same as 1926	10,006	33.00	65.00
1936S	Same	5,006	45.00	125.00
1937D	Oregon Trail Mem., D mint, same as 1926	12,008	31.00	62.50
1938	Oregon Trail Mem., same as 1926	6,006		
1938D	Same	6,005 ⎫ Set		275.00
1938S	Same	6,006 ⎭		
1939	Oregon Trail, same as 1926	3,004		
1939D	Same	3,004 ⎫ Set		375.00
1939S	Same	3,005 ⎭		
	Single type coin		30.00	60.00

1915S	Panama Pacific Exposition, S mint	27,134	100.00	350.00

COMMEMORATIVE SILVER
Pilgrim, Rhode Island, Roanoke, Robinson

		Quan. Available	Abt. Unc.	Unc.
1920	Pilgrim Tercentenary	152,112	$18.00	$26.00
1921	Same	20,053	40.00	75.00

		Quan. Available	Abt. Unc.	Unc.
1936	Rhode Island Tercentenary	20,013		
1936D	Same	15,010 } Set		150.00
1936S	Same	15,011		
	Single type coin		30.00	57.50

		Quan. Available	Abt. Unc.	Unc.
1937	Roanoke Island, N. C., 1587-1937	29,030	45.00	70.00

		Quan. Available	Abt. Unc.	Unc.
1936	Arkansas Centennial (Robinson)	25,265	45.00	55.00

COMMEMORATIVE SILVER

San Diego, Sesquicentennial, Spanish Trail, Stone Mountain

	Quan. Available	Abt. Unc.	Unc.
1935S San Diego, California-Pacific Expo.................. 70,132		$20.00	$35.00
1936D Same... 30,092		25.00	65.00

1926 Sesquicentennial of American Independence 141,120		16.00	27.00

1935 Old Spanish Trail 1535-1935...................... 10,008		325.00	375.00

1925 Stone Mountain Memorial 1,314,709		10.00	15.00

COMMEMORATIVE SILVER
Texas, Vancouver, Vermont

		Quan. Available	Abt. Unc.	Unc.
1934	Texas Centennial	61,463	$25.00	$35.00
1935	Texas Centennial, same as 1934	9,996		
1935D	Same	10,007 } Set		120.00
1935S	Same	10,008		
1936	Texas Centennial, same as 1934	8,911		
1936D	Same	9,039 } Set		120.00
1936S	Same	9,055		
1937	Texas Centennial, same as 1934	6,571		
1937D	Same	6,605 } Set		150.00
1937S	Same	6,637		
1938	Texas Centennial, same as 1934	3,780		
1938D	Same	3,775 } Set		330.00
1938S	Same	3,814		
	Single type coin		25.00	35.00

1925S	Fort Vancouver Centennial	14,994	120.00	260.00

1927	Vermont Sesquicentennial (Bennington)	28,162	65.00	85.00

COMMEMORATIVE SILVER

Washington, B. T., Washington-Carver, Wisconsin

	Quan. Available	Unc.
1946 Booker T. Washington Memorial ...	1,000,546	}Set $15.00
1946D	200,113	
1946S	500,279	
1947	100,017	}Set 30.00
1947D	100,017	
1947S	100,017	
1948	8,005	}Set 60.00
1948D	8,005	
1948S	8,005	

	Quan. Available	Unc.
1949	6,004	}Set $90.00
1949D	6,004	
1949S	6,004	
1950	6,004	}Set 75.00
1950D	6,004	
1950S	512,091	
1951	510,082	}Set 60.00
1951D	7,004	
1951S	7,004	
Single type coin		4.00

1951 Washington-Carver		
	110,018	}Set 32.00
1951D	10,004	
1951S	10,004	
1952	2,006,292	}Set 55.00
1952D	8,006	
1952S	8,006	

1953	8,003	}Set 85.00
1953D	8,003	
1953S	108,020	
1954	12,006	}Set 35.00
1954D	12,006	
1954S	122,024	
Single type coin		4.00

	Quan. Available	Abt. Unc.	Unc.
1936 Wisconsin Centennial	25,015	$60.00	$85.00

COMMEMORATIVE SILVER

York County

	Quan. Available	Abt. Unc.	Unc.
1936 York County, Maine Centennial 25,015		$60.00	$80.00

COMMEMORATIVE GOLD

Grant

1922 Grant Memorial Dollar, star above word "Grant"... 5,016		325.00	725.00
1922 Same, without star................................. 5,000		325.00	725.00

Lewis & Clark

1904 Lewis and Clark Exposition Dollar.................. 10,025		275.00	775.00
1905 Lewis and Clark Exposition Dollar.................. 10,041		275.00	775.00

Louisiana Purchase

1903 Louisiana Purchase Jefferson Dollar 17,500		165.00	300.00
1903 Louisiana Purchase McKinley Dollar................ 17,500		165.00	300.00

McKinley

1916 McKinley Memorial Dollar 9,977		145.00	350.00
1917 McKinley Memorial Dollar 10,000		145.00	350.00

Panama Pacific

1915S Panama Pacific Exposition Dollar................. 15,000		135.00	330.00

COMMEMORATIVE GOLD

Panama Pacific

	Quan. Available	Abt. Unc.	Unc.
1915S Panama Pacific Exposition $2.50	6,749	$500.00	$1,125

1915S Panama Pacific $50 Round	483	—	
1915S Panama Pacific $50 Octagonal	645	—	

Sesquicentennial

1926 Philadelphia Sesquicentennial $2.50	46,019	135.00	220.00

CALIFORNIA FRACTIONAL GOLD PIECES

California gold quarters, halves and dollars are of two kinds:
1. Originals — Made by private companies such as assayers and jewelers in both round and octagonal form. They were made during the gold boom. The denomination spelled DOL. or DOLLAR is found on the genuine pieces. Average premium prices are:

	Ex. Fine	Unc.
Quarter Dollar, Octagonal or Round.	$35.00	$55.00
Half Dollar, Octagonal or Round.	37.50	60.00
Dollar, Octagonal	85.00	150.00
Dollar, Round	425.00	900.00

2. Souvenir specimens do not have the words DOL. or DOLLAR and are worth considerably less than genuine specimens.

RECENT PROOF SETS

Cent—Nickel—Dime—Quarter—Half—(Dollar starting 1973)

Proof coins were not struck during 1943-1949 or 1965-67. Starting in 1973 sets include the dollar coin.
Quantities of proof sets issued are listed in parentheses.

1936	(3,837)	$2,750	1961	(3,028,244)	$6.50
1937	(5,542)	1,700	1962	(3,218,019)	6.50
1938	(8,045)	700.00	1963	(3,075,645)	6.50
1939	(8,795)	650.00	1964	(3,950,762)	7.50
1940	(11,246)	435.00	1968S	(3,041,506)	3.75
1941	(15,287)	430.00	1969S	(2,934,631)	3.75
1942 Both nickels...		500.00	1970S	(2,632,810)	8.50
1942 One nickel .... } (21,120)		430.00	1971S	(3,220,733)	3.75
1950	(51,386)	225.00	1972S	(3,260,996)	4.00
1951	(57,500)	150.00	1973S	(2,760,339)	9.00
1952	(81,980)	75.00	1974S	(2,612,568)	9.00
1953	(128,800)	50.00	1975S	(2,845,450)	17.00
1954	(233,300)	32.00	1976S	(4,149,730)	7.00
1955	(378,200)	25.00	1976S Three piece		
1956	(669,384)	13.00	set	(3,295,714)	12.00
1957	(1,247,952)	8.50	1977S	(3,251,152)	7.50
1958	(875,652)	12.00	1978S	(3,127,781)	19.00
1959	(1,149,291)	8.25	1979S		9.00
1960 Large date .. } (1,691,602)		7.50			
1960 Small date ..		20.00			

UNITED STATES FRACTIONAL CURRENCY

Fractional Currency is paper money issued by the United States government from 1862 to 1875 to relieve the shortage of minor coins. Specimens are still redeemable at their face value at the Treasury Department, Washington, D. C.

FIRST ISSUE

With facsimiles of postage stamps
Perforated Edges (like stamps)

Denomination	V. Fine	E.F.
5¢	$5.00	$17.50
10¢	5.50	17.50
25¢	7.25	20.00
50¢	10.00	22.00

Plain Edges

5¢	1.75	4.00
10¢	1.75	4.00
25¢	2.75	6.50
50¢	5.75	10.00

SECOND ISSUE

(Washington in bronze oval)

5¢	1.50	3.75
10¢	1.50	3.75
25¢	2.25	4.75
50¢	2.75	6.00

THIRD ISSUE

(Green backs)

Denomination	V. Fine	E.F.
3¢ Washington	$2.25	$5.00
5¢ Clark	1.75	5.00
10¢ Washington	1.15	3.50
25¢ Fessenden	2.25	5.25
50¢ Justice	4.50	8.00
50¢ Spinner	3.00	6.00

(Red backs)

5¢ Clark	4.00	10.00
10¢ Washington	2.75	8.00
25¢ Fessenden	2.75	9.00
50¢ Justice	5.00	10.00
50¢ Spinner	4.25	10.00

FOURTH ISSUE

10¢ Liberty	1.10	3.00
15¢ Columbia	5.00	12.00
25¢ Washington	2.25	3.50
50¢ Lincoln	3.25	9.50
50¢ Stanton	2.75	4.00

FIFTH ISSUE

10¢ Meredith	1.10	2.50
25¢ Walker	1.10	3.00
50¢ Dexter	2.25	5.50
50¢ Crawford	2.25	4.00

[125]

COLONIAL COINAGE

The Articles of Confederation, adopted March 1, 1781, provided that Congress should have the sole right to regulate the alloy and value of coin struck by its own authority or by that of the respective states.

Each state, therefore, had the right to coin money, but Congress served as a regulating authority. New Hampshire was the first state to consider coinage, but few if any coins were placed in circulation.

Vermont, Connecticut, and New Jersey granted coining privileges to companies or individuals. Massachusetts erected its own mint in which copper coins were produced. A number of interesting varieties of these state issues, most of which were struck in fairly large quantities, can still be easily acquired, and form the basis for many present day collections of early American coins.

The first Colonial coins struck in this country were the crude "NE Shillings" by the colony of Massachusetts. These pieces were followed by the famous Massachusetts "Pine Tree Shillings" which are dated 1652; this series also included sixpence and threepence pieces of 1652. Dealers buy the more popular Colonial coins at approximately the following prices.

Fine

NE Shilling	$1,500
Massachusetts Pine Tree and Oak Tree Shillings	$125.00
Pine Tree Sixpence ($75.00); Pine Tree Threepence	$100.00
1722-1723 Rosa Americana Coppers	$10.00 to $30.00
1722-1724 Wood's Hibernia Coppers	$3.00 to $10.00
1773 Virginia Halfpenny	$4.50 to $8.00
1776 Continental Dollar	$800.00
1783-1785 Nova Constellatio Coppers	$10.00 to $20.00

1787 Fugio Cent	$15.00
1787-1788 Massachusetts Cent and Half Cent	$8.00 to $10.00
1785 to 1788 Vermont Coppers	$15.00 to $115.00
1786 to 1788 New Jersey Coppers	$5.00 to $25.00
1785-1788 Connecticut Coppers	$4.00 to $25.00
1787 New York Coppers	$20.00 to $150.00
1783-1795 Washington Head Coppers	$10.00 to $50.00
1794-1795 Talbot, Allum and Lee Cent	$4.00 to $10.00

E Pluribus Unum (One composed of many) is the most familiar legend to be found on U.S. Coins. Its equivalent, but with different wording, appeared on money issued prior to the establishment of the mint. Here are a few: A 1776 New York note, "Uno Eodemque Igne" (One and the same fire). One of the Continental notes pictures a harp with 13 strings accompanied by this motto, "Majora Minoribua Consonant" (The greater and the smaller ones sound together). On another note is a circled chain of 13 links and the motto, "We are one."

★　★　★

U. S. COIN STANDARDS

Kinds and denominations of coins	Diameter	Thickness	Standard or gross weight of coins	
	Inches	Inches	Oz. Troy	Grains
SILVER:				
Dollar.........................	1.5	.114	.859375	412.5
Half-dollar	1.205	.086	.401875	192.9
Quarter-dollar	.955	.067	.200937	96.45
Dime	.705	.053	.080375	38.58
CLAD:				
Dollar (Silver)	1.5	.114	.7906	379.5
Dollar (Cop.-Nic.)	1.5	.114	.7292	350.0
Dollar (Cop.-Nic.) Small	1.044	.078	.26041	125.0
Half-dollar (Silver)............	1.205	.086	.369791	177.5
Half-dollar (Cop.-Nic.)	1.205	.086	.3646	175.0
Quarter (Silver)...............	.955	.067	.184870	88.8
Quarter-dollar (Cop.-Nic.)......	.955	.067	.182291	87.5
Dime	.705	.053	.072812	34.95
MINOR:				
Five-cent.....................	.835	.078	.16075	77.16
One-cent	.750	.062	.1	48.0

Kinds and denominations of coins	Weight tolerance (above or below) on individual pieces	Fineness	Fineness tolerance on coinage ingots
	Grains	Thousandths	Thousandths
SILVER:			
Dollar......................	6.0	900	6
Half-dollar	4.0	900	6
Quarter-dollar	3.0	900	6
Dime	1.5	900	6
CLAD:			
Dollar (Silver)	4.0	400	6
Half-dollar (Silver)..........	4.0	400	6
Quarter (Silver)..............	3.0	400	6
Dollar......................	6.0 ⎞		
Half-dollar	4.0 ⎟ 75% copper, 25%	Of cladding,
Quarter-dollar	3.0 ⎟ nickel clad on a	not less than
Dime	1.5 ⎠ core of pure copper	30% of weight
MINOR:			
Five-cent....................	3.0	75% copper; 25% nickel.	Of nickel 25%
One-cent	2.0	95% copper; 5% tin & zinc	Starting 1962- 95% copper; 5% zinc

INDEX

COIN FOLDERS

A Convenient Method of Housing Your Collection

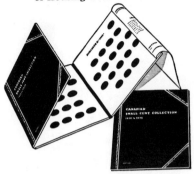

Made by WHITMAN Size Folded 5¾" x 7½"

Made in two tones of blue . . . printed in black and silver, giving a brilliant "Jewel Case" effect to your coin collection.

COMPLETE LIST OF STYLES

UNITED STATES

Large Cent — 1826 to 1857
Indian-Eagle Cents — 1857 to 1909
Lincoln Head Cent — 1909 to 1940
Lincoln Head Cent — 1941-1974
Lincoln Head Cent — Starting 1975
Lincoln Memorial Cent — Starting 1959
Cents — Plain, no printing

Shield Type Nickel — 1866 to 1883
Liberty Head Nickel — 1883 to 1912
Buffalo Nickel — 1913 to 1938
Jefferson Nickel — 1938 to 1961
Jefferson Nickel — Starting 1962
Nickels — Plain, no printing

Barber Dime — 1892 to 1916
Mercury Head Dime — 1916 to 1945
Roosevelt Dime — Starting 1946
Dimes — Plain, no printing

Barber Quarter — 1892 to 1905
Barber Quarter — 1906 to 1916
Lib. Standing Quarter — 1916 to 1930
Wash. Head Quarter — 1932 to 1945
Wash. Head Quarter — 1946 to 1959
Wash. Head Quarter — Starting 1960

Quarters — Plain, no printing

Barber Half Dollar — 1904 to 1915
Lib. Standing Half Dollar — 1916 to 1936
Lib. Standing Half Dollar — 1937 to 1947
Ben. Franklin Half Dollar — 1948 to 1963
Kennedy Half Dollar — Starting 1964
Halves — Plain, no printing

Morgan Dollar — 1878 to 1883
Morgan Dollar — 1884 to 1890
Morgan Dollar — 1891 to 1897
Morgan Dollar — 1898 to 1921
Peace Dollar — 1921 to 1935
Eisenhower Dollar — Starting 1971
Dollars — Plain, no printing

MISCELLANEOUS
20th Century Type Coins

ONE-A-YEAR
Cents, 1909 to Date
Nickels, 1913 to Date
Dimes, 1916 to Date
Quarters, 1916 to Date

U.S. CURRENT ISSUES
Lincoln Cent — Starting 1959
Washington Quarter — Starting 1965

CANADA

Small Cents — 1920 to 1972
Small Cents — Starting 1973
Nickels — 1922-1960
Nickels — Starting 1961
Dimes — 1858 to 1936
Dimes — Starting 1937
Quarters — 1911 to 1952
Quarters — Starting 1953
Quarters — Plain, no printing
Halves — 1870 to 1910
Halves — 1911 to 1936
Halves — 1937-1960
Halves — Starting 1961
Halves — Plain, no printing
Silver Dollars — 1935 to 1957
Silver Dollars — Starting 1958
Dollars — Plain, no printing